The end.

Now what?!

{ 6 STEPS TO TAKE YOUR **MANUSCRIPT** TO **MARKETPLACE** IN 6 WEEKS. }

BY STEVEN SPATZ, PRESIDENT, BOOKBABY

Printed in the United States of America

First Printing, 2014

Print ISBN: 978-1-48356-411-1

AuthorMarketer
37 Darien Way
New Hope, PA 18938

www.AuthorMarketer.com

ACKNOWLEDGEMENTS

I want to thank the dozens of BookBaby authors who emailed, called or told me in person at book conferences how much they enjoyed the guide that inspired this book.

Of course I have to thank my Mom because…well, she's my Mom! She was almost my first editor of all those elementary school essays, and a great one at that. I think she pretty much inspired Step Two.

My only regret is that I can't hand my Dad a copy of this book and see the look of pride in his eye. While he was here on earth he taught me everything I know about having a work ethic. Most importantly he helped me understand how you can apply business principles with compassion and fairness above all.

Very special thanks to my daughters Emma and Sara. They alone knew how important this project was for me both personally and professionally, allowing me the opportunity to spend the necessary hours to put together this book. They offered nothing but encouragement during a very challenging time in all of our lives.

And finally to an often recalled favorite high school English teacher who told me: "Most people have a book or two in them concerning their life's achievements. I think you'll have a couple of dozen."

One down, Mrs. White.

23 to go.

INTRODUCTION

Like so many Americans, one of my favorite modern holiday movies is "A Christmas Story". One scene in the movie is an appropriate way to start our journey. (I assume you've seen the movie; how can you avoid seeing "Christmas Story" when TNT runs it for 24 hours every holiday!)

The scene I'm referencing is when the hero of the story, Ralphie, goes out to the mailbox to discover the long awaited Little Orphan Annie Secret Society Decoder Pin has finally arrived. He rips the package open and then waits for the radio program to broadcast the top-secret coded message.

He runs into the bathroom for a little privacy while he carefully decodes the important message: BE SURE TO DRINK YOUR OVALTINE.

"Ovaltine?" he exclaimed. "A crummy commercial? Son of a bitch!"

Like the Secret Society Pin, this book is intended to help authors to "decode" the publishing process. But while I happen to be the President of BookBaby. com, one of the leading eBook converter and distributors, I can assure you this is not a 100+ page commercial. From time to time I do reference some of the products, services or partners of BookBaby. But the other 99% of this volume is devoted to impartial advice and recommendations over a large range of publishing issues and questions.

If you do want a not so "crummy" commercial, I invite you to go to www. bookbaby.com.

And don't forget to drink your Ovaltine.

The Beginning of The End

I went for years not finishing anything. Because, of course, when you finish something you can be judged. I had pieces that were re-written so many times I suspect it was just a way of avoiding sending them out.
– Erica Jong

Maybe she was having too much fun researching material for her books. But Ms. Jong did indeed finish great works such as *Fear of Flying*, and other landmark books about the sexual revolution.

If you've downloaded or picked up this book, I'm guessing:

1. You've either finished writing one of your own.
2. You're within a few paragraphs and periods of finishing.

For that, I'll say this to you: Congratulations. Next I'll say: Cork the champagne. It's time to go back to work, because some really important work needs to happen next. The process of taking your manuscript beyond the hard drive on your computer can be daunting, to say the least. Many a writer has gone the same route as the early Ms. Jong and let their efforts stall out at this stage. And frankly that's just plain wrong! Your work needs to be read. And that's the purpose of this book – to guide you through the next few steps towards realizing your ultimate goal – seeing your published work in bookstores, both online and off.

Putting together a book of any kind is an achievement, but it's what writers do. However, once they type in "The End" or "Fin" or "конец"… they've simply come to one of many milestones in publishing circa 2015. What follows next is usually outside of an author's comfort zone. This guide is intended to help you take the next steps toward realizing your ultimate goal – seeing your published work in a bookstore, either online or bricks-and-mortar.

But before we go any further we need to ask a question. In this age of technological change and the digital transformation of our society, we need to know something:

Is anyone out there still actually reading books?

Reading in the age of high-tech

Facebook, Twitter, texting, video games, Netflix… there's no shortage of high-tech diversions that eat up the average person's free time these days.

But it seems that Americans are still very interested in a most decidedly low-tech pastime: We still love to read. And that's good news for anyone who's decided to check out this guide.

The latest study from the Pew Research Organization illustrates this nation's enduring love affair with books. Despite the distractions of the latest gizmo or social media site, a constant 75% of those surveyed said they spend several hours per week reading.

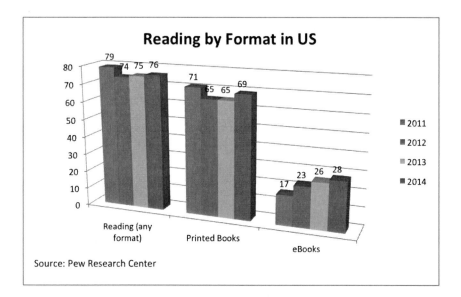

While most still enjoy leafing through the pages of printed books, a growing number of readers are turning to the digital versions. The popularity of eBooks is rising, as millions of readers enjoy new levels of convenience, portability, access, and affordability with their Kindles, iPads, Nooks, tablets, smartphones, and other devices.

Reading snapshot

Among all American adults 18 and older, the % who read at least one book in the following formats in the past year

	Total	Print	E-book	Audiobook
Total (All adults 18+)	**76%**	**69%**	**28%**	**14%**
a Male	69	64	23	14
b Female	82[a]	74[a]	33[a]	15
Race/ethnicity				
a White	76	71[c]	29[c]	14
b Black	81[c]	75[c]	30[c]	19
c Hispanic	67	56	16	14
Age group				
a 18-29	79	73	37[cd]	15
b 30-49	75	66	32[d]	16
c 50-64	77	71	27[d]	16
d 65+	70	66	12	10
Education level				
a High school grad or less	64	57	14	10
b Some college	83[a]	78[a]	32[a]	15[a]
c College graduate	88[a]	78[a]	45[ab]	21[a]
Household income				
a < $30,000	68	63	14	12
b $30,000-$49,999	75	70	28[a]	16
c $50,000-$74,999	85[a]	78[a]	42[ab]	19
d $75,000+	83[a]	74[a]	46[ab]	14
Community type				
a Urban	77	71	29[c]	15
b Suburban	75	67	31[c]	14
c Rural	76	72	18	14

Note: Columns marked with a superscript letter (*) or another letter indicate a statistically significant difference between that row and the row designated by that superscript letter. Statistical significance is determined inside the specific section covering each demographic trait.

Source: Pew Research Center's Internet Project Omnibus Survey, January 2-5, 2014. N= 1005 American adults ages 18 and older. Interviews were conducted on landlines and cell phones, in English and Spanish.

PEW RESEARCH CENTER

Though eBooks are rising in popularity, print remains the foundation of Americans' reading habits: Among adults who read at least one book in the past year, just 5% said they read an eBook in the last year without also reading a print book. In general, the vast majority of those who read eBooks and audiobooks also read print books.

So what does this mean to the aspiring author? Simply this – it's your time!

The era of the Author

Beyond the exploding sales numbers, the electronic publishing age offers opportunities for new and prospective authors that have previously been open to a select few.

Authors in control – Society's creative types — artists, musicians, sculptors, and authors — have almost always been at the mercy of others controlling and profiting from their art. It's been that way since Michelangelo was painting ceilings in Rome. A couple of careers ago, I had a business partner who was a very talented artist and sculptor. For years he had worked for companies like Franklin Mint and Hasbro, toiling away on making models and prototypes of action figures and collectibles. Some of the pieces he created have sold millions of copies over the years. Mind you, my friend was well paid for his efforts. But he never saw the real financial windfall for his creations because he never had access to the marketplace in a substantial way. In those pre-Internet days, large collectible companies controlled access to retailers and later to direct marketers like QVC. Today everyone has access to the marketplace through websites like eBay and etsy.com. Sure enough, today my ex-partner is now creating and selling artwork directly to collectors – and making about 10X as much money as before.

With eBooks, authors can finally have as much control as they want because of their direct access to their reading audience. By retaining all electronic rights to their eBooks, authors can dictate when and where their books are available for sale.

Short timeline – In the "publisher in control" model, when an author finally completes his or her manuscript, it's a classic case of hurry-up-and-wait. Let's go through the steps.

Most publishers insist that you submit your manuscript through a literary agent. Finding the right agent for your book can take months of query letters. It's quite possible the agent will want to take your book to another editor to reposition the text. More time goes by.

Then you'll need to hammer out a contract with him or her. That means phone conference calls, trips to your lawyer's office and a few more weeks burned.

Then more weeks pass as you work together to hone an acceptable "pitch" that the agent will send to publishers. Perhaps there is more culling through the lists of publishers to pitch. More days go by.

Next come months—maybe a year or more—of submissions to publishers. And even though you've invested months – maybe even a year at this point – into the process thus far, it's far from certain that you'll find anyone to publish your work. It's a gamble.

For the sake of this timeline, let's say your agent hits pay dirt and corrals an interested publisher. Then things really slow down! Weeks of contract negotiations follow. The publisher may insist on more rewrites and editing.

Finally, after months of preparing the perfect manuscript, your book goes onto their publishing schedule, along with the dozens of other books accepted that month, behind the hundreds already on the schedule. Due to lead times, it could be another year to 18 months before the book rolls off the press or is available for download.

The bottom line: the really lucky authors who manage to emerge from this traditional publishing gauntlet are looking at a minimum of two years from the time they start their author query to the time they see their hard work on a local bookstore shelf. In that same 24 months, you could have had multiple books self-published, established your author marketing platforms, attracted legions of loyal readers and banked some sales. It's a simple choice: You can self-publish your eBook and have it listed on Amazon in a few weeks or gamble that you're that one in a thousand authors who will find a traditional publishing deal in a couple of years.

Let the marketplace decide – OK, so you might be biased about your own literary efforts. But do you really want to bet your writing career on the whims and opinions of a literary agent who reads dozens of manuscripts each week? And that's if you can even manage to get their attention at all.

Authors who have decided to self-publish spend their time publishing – getting their books directly into the hands of readers all over the world. The reading public is a much better judge of talent because they vote with their wallets!

Special interests can be special – So you've spent years of your life writing your opus: Thursday Morning Mating Habits of Left-Winged Emperor Penguins. Try getting a traditional publisher to commit the resources to print it. With eBooks, even tiny niche titles are economical to produce, satisfying small yet potentially profitable reading audiences.

Last but certainly not least:

More bank – The old payment formulas are completely upside down in the eBook world. Instead of accepting miniscule royalty percentages going through old school publishers, authors are seeing up to 70% of sales receipts through some of the online retailers. Even when eBook authors bring prices way down to 2.99…$1.99…even $.99…they're realizing much higher revenue totals because of increased unit sales.

It's time

Time to get personal for a second: Like so many of you I had dreams of being a published author. But as I became more immersed in my marketing career I couldn't find the time to devote to pursuing a publishing deal, let alone an agent query. So what happened? The opportunity came to me. With the proliferation of smart phones, tablets and e-readers came the self-publishing revolution. My goal was finally within reach, thanks largely to the power of the Internet.

We're enjoying a truly revolutionary time, when technology is enabling us to create and deliver our stories, opinions and – in my case – professional advice in so many new ways. As I write this, more people still buy physical books than eBooks (currently eBook penetration is at about 25%), but that equation is equalizing more and more every day and is sure to reverse itself in the next few years. And yet even the barriers that used to exist to seeing your words in print, hardbound paper and ink has gone away. Once the domain of vanity press, digital printing and POD (print on demand) have expanded our horizons.

While I applaud and encourage those who continue to shoot for the traditional publishing deal with all of the trimmings and prestige, our new shared opportunity is mostly centered on self-publishing. Digital delivery systems such as Apple's iBooks and Amazon's Kindle Direct Publishing bring your readers right to your doorstep. Almost overnight, self-publishing, which was once a stigma associated with failure, has come to be regarded as a badge of honor.

And while the party has already started, we're still at the very beginning. The digital technology driving this publishing revolution is enabling creative people around the globe to develop and market content in truly unique ways. Much has been made of the line "content is king", the phrase first coined by Bill Gates back in the practically prehistoric year of 1996. And yet this thesis first offered 20 years ago is proving to be prophetic. New mediums are being invented and old ones are being re-invented. New devices are being created at unprecedented rates. Whether it's blogging or social media, with its vast reach, or a still unthought-of combination of interactive technologies, it still returns to the same starting point. The very same one, in fact, that powered the first movable type printing press: content. Unique and marvelous, informative and inspiring. Your stories, opinions, thoughts and experiences brought into the marketplace, in search of readers. That's our job for the next half dozen weeks.

Our six-week march

I've written this book for the ambitious author who is ready to put some time and even more effort into making their book into the best it can be at this stage. I add that modifier – "at this stage" – because the content of your book is pretty much set. Yes, there will be tinkering and tweaking, not to mention editing. But 95% of your writing is finished. What we're going to do over the next few weeks is help your book realize its vast potential. Some of the steps we take might be outside your area of expertise, if not your comfort zone. Don't worry – we'll get through it together!

That said, let's explore the six steps you have to take to bring your manuscript to the marketplace in six weeks or so. In order they are:

Finishing strong– Knowing when you're really finished with your book. Remember those timed tests in grade school where, at the end of the period, the teacher barked out: "PENCILS DOWN"? This kind of hard stop is what you need for your book, and we'll discuss some various techniques and ideas to help you know when done IS done.

Essential Editing – We'll go through some of the reasons why editing your book is essential. Finding an editor is easy; finding the editor that's right for you might be a challenge. We'll explore where and how to look for your partner in writing crime, even if you don't have a budget for it.

Choosing the publishing pathway – Do you chase your dream of pursuing the traditional "book deal" and all the trappings? Or do you take your career into your own hands and self-publish? We'll review the pros and cons and help you to make up your mind.

Marketing Musts – Authors love to write but marketing? Not so much. But it's an evil that is necessary and we'll help you get a jump start on marketing basics. While book promotion usually gets all the attention, we'll spend time in areas that are often overlooked in the marketing mix.

Creating the Killer Cover – You've spent months – maybe even years – crafting words into your book. Now it needs the perfect packaging – an eye-catching book cover. We'll review some design basics and recommendations for that all important visual.

Picking your product – Will it be old school printed books? Or new school eBooks? Or perhaps both? We'll finish out your publishing journey with a comparison between the formats, along with some file formatting basics to help your project go smoother.

It's a forced march to be sure, but it's one that any motivated author can finish. Depending on the path you choose, you can be seeing your eBook up for sale at Amazon, iBooks, Barnes & Noble, and other stores a few short weeks from today.

Let's get going!

Step 1 – When is done really done?

Typing "The End" is no guarantee that you're finished.

TIMELINE: 1 WEEK

Finishing a book is just like you took a child out in the back yard and shot it.
–Truman Capote

Now that's what I call starting this six week journey off with a bang! But Capote was only expressing the thoughts of many authors who feel a sense of tangible loss at the end of their story. The prospect of this sudden void in their lives has led to far too many books being "overcooked".

I've used that metaphor deliberately to help illustrate my point. When I venture into the kitchen to create something for the family, my kids often laugh at the slavish way I follow each and every line on the recipe. Most importantly, I pay close attention to the instructions that tell you when the food is actually "done".

Want that steak medium rare? I've got a little thermometer gauge that tells me when it's reached 155 degrees. Are the brownies done yet? Stick a toothpick in. If it comes out clean – they're done.

Most authors probably wish they had a gauge of some kind to stick into the pages of their book to tell them it's done. It's not just new, inexperienced writers who have that wish. Most published authors that I've posed the question to say the same thing. It's hard to know when to put down the virtual pen. Sure, today's digital publishing and eBooks allow for change that was never possible in the analog printed book world pre-2008. But it's human nature to want to constantly improve and tinker with your work. Most authors say if allowed to pick up their work again six months after finishing, they'll find more than a few things to change beyond some simple typo fixes.

But there's a difference between people reading this guide and the ones who are looking at their Amazon sales every day: They finished. They walked away from their book despite the fact it wasn't a perfect piece of prose – no book is. My boss said something to me a couple of months ago that really stuck with me: Don't let great be the enemy of good. For the now-published authors, it was good enough to go to the next step.

We're on a six-week long journey and our purpose in this kick-off week of our journey together is help you know it's time to take that next step forward. In this chapter we will:

- Discuss some of the "soft" signs your book is finished, based on experiences from other authors including myself. You may recognize some or all of these signs that you're near the end of the road.

- Cover some very specific steps you can take to determine if you're finished writing. Some of these will take time to complete, but that's what this week is for.

- Go over some of the technical issues of your now "finished" book, including a word-count guide and some simple pre-editing tasks that can save you time and money.

Some signs pointing to the finish line

We're trying to get your book in shape for the editing it richly deserves – and frankly needs. This chapter isn't about fixing those typos or sentence structure. It's about making sure your book is telling the story you want told, in the way you want it told, and in a way that can make sense to thousands of potential readers. For that to happen, you as the author need to be ready to put down the "pen". So to give you some clues if your own book is "done", here are some "toothpicks" and "thermometers" so that you can gauge the doneness of your book:

From red to white – One BookBaby author I interviewed for this book uses color to illustrate the progress of his books. After what he calls his "last draft" he prints out the pages once again and does some serious self-editing. He uses a bright red sharpie and lays into the pages. After a first ruthless editing, he says the pages look like they're hemorrhaging, a sea of red. A draft later it's just a few red slashes. Finally, he says, he's looking at pages with only the occasional slashes of red. He says to see the progress before his eyes is a satisfying way to know that the book is finally turning into the story he intended to tell.

So obvious… So boring! – I've encountered this myself. On this book even! Authors tell me how sick they get of their precious book. They get to a point where they know more about the plot and storyline of their fictional characters than real life family and colleagues. Of course you should – these are the "people" you've been living with for the past weeks and months. You have to believe in your original sense of humor that made you think that joke was funny.

Remember, it's new to your reader, so it will take a bit of self control not to delete them all. It's the same with your plot. Long ago when you embarked on this book project, you thought your plot was marvelous. It still is! You have the curse of knowing where the story leads and ends.

The truth is: The jokes ARE hilarious, as good as the first time you typed them. The plot IS spellbinding; the twists and turns are sure to please. The information I'm relaying in this book IS solid, professional self-publishing advice. We writers are just bored. Which is a sure sign that it's time to move on.

Changing for change's sake – Look at the last few changes you've made to your book. Did you improve it? Or did you just change it? You're not adding value to your book at this point. You're not making it more interesting or richer or even more readable. You're delaying the inevitable. There comes a point when the longer you revise, the less return you're going to get for your effort. You've reached a point of diminishing return.

A new story – Every writer has ideas for that next book, or more likely books. Maybe there have been big changes in your life and you're not in the same emotional place as you were when you started this book. Whatever the reason, your enthusiasm for this current project may be waning. For you to simply say, "I don't feel like writing this story anymore" is an important sign you can't ignore. When you lose interest in the book, you'll stop caring. Your reader will know – who hasn't read a book where it felt like the writer just lost interest in the project and wrapped it up in an all too fast and unsatisfying manner?

You're about to enter into a new relationship – actually multiple relationships – with your readers. The reader has entered into the relationship with optimism and interest in your prose. You're obligated to honor your commitment to entertaining, informing and delighting your new BFFs. They're very excited about reading your book. If you aren't as excited about adding any more to the story, it's a sure sign that you're actually damaging your book rather than enhancing it.

Put your book to the test

It's always good to get some second and third opinions on your book, just as long as they're not people you spend the holidays with. You should pretty much ignore the comments and less-than-critical critiques from your close friends and family. Beware the praises or critiques of your great-aunt Edna. Few friends or family members can honestly offer you objective feedback. If they CAN, count yourself lucky and listen to what they have to say.

In most cases, you'd be better off joining a local writers group. The authors in these groups can provide tremendous feedback, inspire new ideas, and give great moral support. Writing is often a very solitary pursuit and these groups can be your lifeline at times. Digest their commentary, be surprised at their insights and your blind spots, dust yourself off and revise if necessary. It really is a great suggestion…for your next book. On our 42-day-long march, there's not a lot of time for building up new connections.

Online help – The Internet can be a force of good or evil, depending on what you're looking for. The web can be a virtual lifeline for writers who toil in relative isolation. As I said above, it's probably too late for you to really take advantage of the hundreds of websites, forums and discussion groups where you can interact directly with writers like you, plus editors and others in the publishing industry. When you do have the time it's bound to be a worthwhile experience for you to submit writing samples for an honest critique. Many provide an extremely creative environment for authors, offering hundreds of unique writing tools and opportunities for creation and inspiration. You may very well be surprised at their insights and help in pointing out your blind spots. Some of the criticism can be pretty strong, so be prepared for the honest – and sometimes brutal – comments. After absorbing what they have to say, you'll need to dust yourself off and take the criticism for what it's worth.

Here are a few sites worth checking out while you're starting the process for your next book:

- Writers Café (www.writerscafe.org/)
- World Literary Café (http://www.worldliterarycafe.com/forum/35)
- Authonomy (www.authonomy.com)

…and there are dozens more online.

Read your book like its brand new – Every guide like this has the same advice. While it is completely unoriginal, you can take this to mean: It must be damn good advice! You've spent hundreds of hours looking bleary-eyed at the characters on a screen. Take it offline for another look.

Find yourself a bright highlighter and sit down to read it through as though you're a reader. Whenever you find a phrase, a sentence, whenever you want to change/fix something, make a mark and move on. Do not stop to do an edit. Once you get to 'the end' you can go back to your file, start at the last page and work backward, making changes and corrections.

Print a second hard copy, but this time change the font to something visually quite different. If you work in Times New Roman, try printing in Calibri. You'll see it looks very different and you may be surprised by how many little typos, etc., you manage to catch.

You can also trick your eye to see things you've missed before by using a colored font. Better still, go find some pastel colored paper and print it out. If you're concerned about trees or the cost of ink, change your line spacing of 1.5 or 1.15 and use narrow margins. Also, when you print the second hard copy, use the back side of the first.

Last comes first – On the next run-through, read your manuscript. No, not word for word starting with "End The". Do it a chapter at a time. Read the last chapter, then the next to last and so on until you reach the first. This serves to take things out of context for you and you won't be as likely to skim over what you expect to be there. It might feel uncomfortable, but authors report that it works.

Read it. Write it. Speak it – When my kids were slogging through high school, I used to tell them time and again: The best way to master a subject is to learn by the power of three. Read the material. Write notes about the topic you've just read. Then speak it out loud. So get some throat lozenges and find a quiet room. Reading your book aloud can also help you see it fresh and let you more easily identify awkward phrases or sentences.

Distill your book in summaries – This is a tactic borrowed from the visual art world. The usual assignment is to draw quick sketches of an everyday item. Let's say for the purpose of this illustration that you are assigned to draw a toaster. And draw it again and again. A total of 25 times, in 25 different ways. You'd have to get very creative, maybe sketch it from different perspectives or angles, maybe with props or decorations.

Now apply this same task to testing out your book. The assignment is to write a series of summaries about your book plot from different perspectives or viewpoints. You don't need to write out 25 – maybe 10 would suffice. These can be pretty short pieces, but these few words can be very powerful in helping you to understand the real essence of the book. Or at least what you as the author believe it to be. You can complete them over a few days, giving you a chance to put them away for a day or so. Then pick them up and read them back-to-back. Are they consistent? Are the plotlines sound? Are the relative strengths of your characters or topics sound? Perhaps these summaries will provide clues about how to best structure your book.

Final tip from a "pro"

The last trick of the trade I'll share with you is courtesy of Dani Shapiro, the critically acclaimed author of *Slow Motion and Devotion*. She has also written for magazines such as The New Yorker, The Oprah Magazine, Vogue, and

ELLE. Shapiro gave the keynote address at a recent Writer's Digest Conference in New York and shared an interesting technique she uses to help her understand when her book is finished.

Shapiro helped put things into context as she described the simple process of sending an email. When you're composing the note, the words and thoughts express a certain position or point of view. Everything looks right and so you hit: Send.

Immediately after the electrons fly through the ether, you see it: that obvious typo. The one you looked right past 10 times as the author. But what really happened is that the minute you hit the send button you read the message as a completely different person – the recipient.

This is the approach she takes when takes that last critical examination of her book. She actually reads the book as if she's someone else. She'll read chapters as if she's a kindly caring person on one day. On another she reads it as an angry critical person. From the readings of these and other personas, Shapiro is satisfied that her diverse audience is ready to read her next book.

Before the handoff

In the next chapter we'll discuss the need for your book to undergo intensive editing. Before we get there, here's a final checklist of common simple proofreading problems that befall almost every author. If you take care of as many of these issues as possible on your own, it can save you some time AND money in terms of less work for your editor:

- Find/Replace double-space with single space – There is no reason that comes to mind where you'd want multiple spaces in a row. If there is in your work, just make a note of it and go back to fix it. Note: if you're paranoid that you left three spaces in a row somewhere, just do this twice.

- Find/Replace period-space-quote with just period-quote – You can accidentally insert a space between a period and a quote as you write. Maybe you deleted a word at the end, or maybe you just got trigger-happy on the spacebar. We're not here to judge.

- Add proper nouns to your spell checker, including possessive forms and adjective forms (if you've made up place names, for example). Misspellings of proper nouns are tough on your editor. They're not as familiar with these names as you are, and there's no dictionary to check them against. If you go 50/50 on spelling for a name, they may not even be able to tell which is the correct spelling.

- Though/through/thought – Do a search for each of these. It's time-consuming, but these are easy words to mix up, since they're common, long (compared to articles, not chemical or disease names). Make sure the right word is used in context.

- They're/there/their – Same for these friendly homonyms.

- It's/ its – Depending how good you are with this one, you might only need to search for one or the other, but searching through for both is safest.

- A/An – OK, this one sounds daunting, but there's a trick. You only care about using "a" when a vowel follows, so search for " a a", " a e", " a i", " a o", and " a u". Remember the preceding space, so you don't catch words that just end in "a". You can do the same for "an" and all the consonants. If it sounds like a lot of work, consider reading through your whole manuscript and looking for them while also looking for anything else that might be wrong.

- Further/Farther – This is really getting into personal issues now. Everyone is going to have their own particular words or word groupings that they routinely mistype.

If you're not sure which you have problems with, I suggest you look through this list of the most commonly misused words: http://wsuonline.weber.edu/wrh/words.htm

Length matters

One simple way to tell if your book done is the number of words you've put to paper. It's a crude yet important measuring stick, and easy way to tell if your books is too long or too short, based upon genre and type.

You can use the generally agreed upon standard below to see where your book falls:

- Short stories – generally 1000 – 8000 words

- Novella – 10,000-30,000 words

- Commercial Fiction (including women's fiction, crime fiction, fantasy etc) 95,000-120,000 words

- Romance category – 55,000– 85,000 words

- Non-fiction – wide variance by subject matter

For children's books:

- Board Book — 100 words maximum

- Early Picture book — 500

- Picture book — 750- 1,000 words maximum

- Early Reader — 3,500 words is an absolute maximum

- Chapter book — 10,000 words

- Middle Grade — 35,000 words for contemporary, mystery, humor; 45,000 for fantasy/sci-fi, adventure and historical

- YA — 70,000 words for contemporary, humor, mystery, historical, romance, etc.; 90,000 words for fantasy, sci-fi, paranormal, etc.

Stay within the limits for your genre. This is the amount of content that your would-be readers are expecting. If your book is too long or too short you will have difficulty finding readers.

Keep writing. Keep abandoning.

"Art is never finished," said Leonardo DaVinci. "It is abandoned." How do you know when to abandon your book and move on to the next step? Revisions can be like dirty laundry - never ending if you allow it.

As always, there are no rules when it comes to calling your novel, self-help book or memoir complete. It's up to you to make that decision. The more you write, the better you'll become at knowing when your time is up with a particular story or topic. So keep writing and keep abandoning. When you look back at what you've created, you'll see the mistakes you made; you'll see where you gave up too early. And hopefully, you'll learn from it.

For me as a writer, there are different degrees of being "finished." I mentioned my final draft above. That's when I think my book is finished enough for a ruthless self-editing. Before I get to this stage I'm feeling pretty confident that I can at least take my book to the next level of "finished." To me that's the point where the first set of eyes that don't belong to me gets the privilege (or torture) of looking at my still pretty raw writing. And that's where your timeline could easily be thrown out the window.

When you finally open up the kimono and allow others to read your precious words, they might raise questions you'd never dreamed could be asked about your plot or make inferences about your characters that you hadn't a clue were possible – and you'll feel like you're back to square one. Do you take their advice? At the very least they've raised issues and perhaps doubt about your book. You may not want to accept their advice but at the very least you should now consider a third opinion. And probably a fourth, fifth and sixth.

My hope is that you won't be one of those people who refine the same book forever. In reality they are just avoiding taking the step of letting others look at their work. Perhaps they're polishing so much it's down to the bare metal. Or they're constantly reinventing their style by redoing the same story when they should start a new one.

As writers we're learning and changing all the time. We write our books according to the writer we are at the moment. With every subsequent manuscript you write, you're improving as an author. Most published authors develop an inner sense of rightness. They know that their book will generally be ready after the third draft, or the fifth, or however many drafts it usually takes.

When you've been through the process a few times, you'll have an easier time knowing when your story is done. You won't be able to explain it, but you'll know. You'll know that your novel is as good as you can make it.

A lot of other writing experts have this to say about completing a book: "In reality, a book is finished when everybody is reasonably happy." Usually the "everybody" is people involved in the traditional publishing process – an agent, editor, publisher, publicist…and of course the author. They are usually different people playing different roles in the process of producing the book.

I'm guessing that your version of "everybody" is quite different. Your team is composed of you as the author, you as the husband/wife/father/mother, you as the (insert your career or academic path). In this scenario, these different roles or responsibilities are going to reside in one person – you. On the one hand, you love your story and want it to be the best it can possibly be. On the other, there comes a time when your other responsibilities demand the time previously spent typing on your keyboard.

Time's up. Pens down. You've got a deadline.

Maybe the best test of all that it's time to move on is nothing having to do with the words on the pages. Maybe it's the ticking of a clock. As I sit here typing this on a Saturday morning, I've put myself into a self-imposed deadline to have this finished by Monday morning.

Because that's the deadline I've imposed upon myself to hand this project off to the people discussed in the next chapter. I'll be putting my 30,000 or so well-chosen words into the hands of people who might absolutely crush them with an editing pen.

Step 2 – Editing is for everyone.

Without editing, even a good book could be doomed.

TIMELINE: 4 WEEKS

It is perfectly okay to write garbage —as long as you edit brilliantly.
- -C. J. Cherryh

I can't say it strongly enough: Editing is an absolute must if you want your book to reach its full potential. There isn't a writer on this planet that doesn't benefit from some level of editing. That includes me and you. (Editor's note – especially this guy.) I'm pretty certain Moses was coming down from Mt. Sinai with 14 Commandments until divine editing intervened to make the final product more concise, punchy and above all, memorable.

This modest little book is no exception. Now that I've gone on the record about the need for editing, I'm living in mortal fear that someone, somewhere is going to find a typo and misspelling. Look, typos happen to the best of us – and I'm surely not in that company. But as I write these words and proceed to my final draft, I fully expect them to be tweaked, modified, changed, scratched out…and made better by the efforts of a skilled editor. I can hardly wait!

Errors can make the writer appear uneducated and unprofessional. Let's say the book is something that helps promote your career or business. If the author is careless about what he or she publishes, readers may wonder if he or she is as careless with the products or services provided.

Correcting these kinds of errors is just one level of editing. Sentences, paragraphs, and pages need to work together. People with good English grammar don't necessarily have the skills or training to organize and present content well. If key points are missing, buried, or unclear, readers may not keep reading. And the relationship is over.

Editors will also check for consistency in the story, for repetitions, flow, rhythm and transitional phrases. They will check on tone and tense, and will provide suggestions on certain parts that do not read well. They can be asked to check facts and statistics.

But be prepared: Editing is going to cost you something out of pocket. Is this a question of "you get what you pay for?" Not necessarily. For those on a Ramen Noodle budget when it comes to your book – do not despair! There are some free online options for you to use, and we'll cover those later in the chapter.

But consider this: Not editing has its own hidden costs. Poor grammar will drive away readers, agents, potential reviews. Your book could be chock full of grammar, punctuation, and spelling errors that will jerk readers out of the reading experience. It's the editor's job to find and fix those errors.

Editing is an investment matched only by the investment of your hard work and time getting the book to this point. Whatever you end up paying for an outside editor, it's going to be worth it.

In this chapter we will:

- Outline the types of editing your book might require, from simple proofreading to substantial plot revisions and reviews.

- Help you start your search for the perfect editor. Where do you find them? And how do you determine if they are going to be a good fit for your book?

- Review the economics of editing, including some surprisingly effective and economical alternatives for those with a tight budget.

On our timeline, we're going to allow four weeks for this process, from finding your editor to getting back your fully edited manuscript. If you're scoring at home, that means we've only tackled two items on the list and we're already five weeks into our six week process. Relax – there are three steps we can be working on while your manuscript is being edited. But more on that later…

Determine the Type of Editing You Need

Proofreading. Line Editing. Content Editing. There are all kinds and flavors of editing to choose from, and price tags to match. What do they entail? Let's try to sort out and explain the different levels of editing, starting with the most basic and working our way up:

- Proofreading – It's also called 'word level' editing and is the simplest form of editing. It's also usually the cheapest. Proofreading is for writers who don't need help with sentence structure or the content of the book itself, but need someone to simply go over the text for basic grammatical and spelling errors. It usually takes an editor about two weeks to proofread a full-length manuscript. The purpose of proofreading is to have someone who has never read your manuscript go over each word for errors that might have escaped your attention, which will happen at least a few times in a full-length manuscript. It's the simple stuff: Their-They're-There kind of things. A lot of these errors are found using an online spell check of course, but I wouldn't trust my final product with it.

- Copy Editing – Also known as 'sentence level' editing, this is the most popular type of editing offered. It's a bit more detailed than proofreading as it addresses grammar, usage and consistency issues. I'd also call it "Quality Control" editing because of the small-yet-critical details that are checked over. For instance, what if the writer calls out the woman's deep, penetrating blue-green eyes on page 27, but by page 336 they've turned into a dazzling emerald color? Your copy editor should be able to spot that error. Maybe it's a story detail – a town name, the name of pet in the plot – that's mentioned 24 times. A line editor makes sure it's the same each of those 24 occasions. So in addition to consistencies in spelling and punctuation (colour or color?), a copyeditor is paid to find issues of continuity that don't add up.

- Line editing – Also called stylistic or paragraph editing, this kind of editing takes it up a notch above pure grammar issues. A good line editor can recast sentences for clarity and flow, or move sentences around so that your meaning is clear. Stylistic editing always aims to preserve the author's voice, first and foremost. Line editors also deal with sentence length, excessive use of adjectives, use of jargon or a vocabulary level that doesn't match the target audience. If you think your manuscript is basically complete but might have plot holes, limited characterization, factual errors or syntactical problems, line editing is probably what you need. A great line editor can help with those all important paragraph transitions that can make a book stilted. The purpose of line editing is to tie together loose ends in your manuscript and to make sure that the story flows properly, and has the rhythm and pulse that readers enjoy in a well written AND edited story. For non-fiction, line editing will catch factual errors and will also help to separate chapters and paragraphs so that they make more sense.

- Substantive Editing – This is sometimes called developmental or big-picture editing. A substantive edit can be fairly expensive, and often involves the rearranging, deleting, adding and rewording of entire pages and chapters. Every book has its trouble spots – maybe the plot is lost in reams of background information. Perhaps the characters are difficult to distinguish from one another. This level of editing has less to do with the mechanics of the book than the psyche of the manuscript. Many books are improved when large chunks of text are moved around, and possibly through cutting some sections as well. This editor addresses the structure of a book — how everything hangs together.

If your book requires a substantive edit, you should probably forget about our 6 week timeline right now and get it into order. It can be very expensive if you need to address a book's structure after it has been completely written.

The cheapest way to address big-picture conflicts is to get help addressing the problem before you spend much time writing it. Want to know for sure? Then try this: Send your most trusted friend in the writing community a detailed outline or plot summary to see if any potential holes come to light.

There oughta be a match.com for editors.

There are no shortage of resources available for you to find the editor that suits your needs. Caution: Everybody with an English degree or who teaches high school English thinks they can be a great editor. Editing is an underrated talent, a combination of skill, understanding of the genre, and appreciation of a writer's style.

A quick Google search will yield hundreds of choices. Many authors I've talked to have found editors by browsing the listings at leading industry sites such as Writer's Digest's (www.writersdigest.com) or Media Bistro. (www.mediabistro.com). Editors who advertise on these sites have, at the very least, decided to spend a little money to promote their services. It's a low bar for these alleged wordsmiths to jump over, but at least it's some kind of bar.

Or you can go even lower: I've heard of authors having great luck using good ol' Craig's List. (www.craigslist.org). I'm not saying it's necessarily a bad place to find an editor if you ultimately go that route. But that place is a jungle, with a lot of scammers and just plain lousy editors sprinkled in amongst the quality choices. Go ahead – take a look for yourself. And then go to some more trusted places to start your search.

I'd start my search with the Editorial Freelancer's Association website (http://www.the-efa.org/). This group is well-respected in the publishing world. The site directory is full of paying members, meaning they've made the small investment to establish legitimacy in this field. EFA members are editors, writers, indexers, proofreaders, researchers, desktop publishers, translators, and others who offer a broad range of skills and specialties.

You can search through the extensive online EFA job listing service, which offers clients another way to find the right freelancer for the job. It's a pretty good site to simply explore, as EFA also provides resources for both freelancers and clients. At the site you can access things such as guidelines for hiring and working with editors, and a job list where you can post your project. The EFA also has a great list of typical rates for various kinds of editorial services at http://www.the-efa.org/res/rates.php.

For our neighbors north of the border, try the Editors' Association of Canada (http://www.editors.ca/). And across the pond in the UK, the best option is Society for Editors and Proofreaders (http://www.sfep.org.uk/).

Social media platforms like LinkedIn remain one of the best gathering spots for industry professionals. You can search the sites to find dozens of user groups or communities within the publishing world, such as:

- Publishing and Editing Professionals
- Writing and Editing Professionals
- Freelance Editing Network

If money is no object, go to your own bookshelf and look at some recent books. Check the acknowledgments in well-written books, as editors are usually listed there. But let's be realistic: The editors of best-selling books or those published by the Big 5 publishers might be out of your price range. You can try some regionally published books, if possible, as well as books published by partner publishers or small presses, since they tend to work heavily with freelance editors.

Full disclosure: I'm having my book edited by the fine folks at FirstEditing. com. After vetting dozens of groups of editors a few years ago, BookBaby chose this group as its preferred book editors. They're fast and affordable, with a large group of editors that are well matched to all of the popular genres.

Editing your list of editors

What do you look for in an editor? Most editors concentrate on one or a few genres, and that's a good thing. I don't think I'd want a Young Adult book editor to help me with a text about marketing! So start your search for an editor that's experienced with your type of subject matter.

Here are some of the best ways to aid in your search for the right editor:

Get a sample edit – Before you buy a car, you always take a test drive. It's the same with editing. If you're going to invest a good sum of money into this service, you need to be confident they can deliver an amazing final product. Many freelance editors are, or should be, willing to give you a free sample edit. The company that partners with BookBaby for editing services – Firstediting.com – gives authors a free edit of the first chapter of their book within 24 hours, along with a price quote for editing the whole book.

Where in the world are they? – If your editor is somewhere like Taiwan or New Zealand, their cost of living might be far less than an editor living and working in the US. Like all self-employed people, editors price accordingly to what they need where they live. If an editor lives in a very expensive city or area of the world, they will charge more. One more point about location: Find an editor who speaks your kind of English. They aren't all the same; even a lot of the spelling differs. For mass-market, broad appeal, Canadian/American English is best.

Education and experience – Don't overpay for this. Unless you're looking for a substantial rewrite, having an editor with a PhD in Literature doesn't necessarily mean they edit well. Editors should charge based on how fast they think they can get the work done. Translated: How much do I need to charge to make it worth my while? Fancy titles or diplomas should not merit bonus payment. Don't get carried away by their resume; pay attention to their skills.

In praise of youth - The editor who advertises "28 years of professional editing" isn't necessarily the best candidate. Editing is exhausting – you need sharp eyes, lots of caffeine, an ability to concentrate and a keen intelligence. At the risk of age discrimination, I'd probably pick someone in the 23-33 age range. You don't need to come out and ask, "How old are you?" You can figure it out from their resume.

Are they writers? – Just because a prospective editor claims to be a writer himself, that doesn't give him an edge over the editor who focuses on nothing but editing others' work. Yet having the perspective of the writer can be an asset. If they've written a book start to finish, they're probably more aware of what it takes to write one. Ask the editor in question to share the books they've written. Get a Kindle sample and see if the writing is clean and excellent.

Is their website hideous? – Anyone who's taking their business seriously knows the importance of having a clean, professional website. There's just no good reason for an editor's website to look like something out of 1999. Is this a professional calling or are they just doing editing as a retirement income or hobby?

Working your short list

Once you've narrowed your search to 3-4 likely prospects, it's time to make contact. Every editor has their preferred way to discuss new projects. When you introduce yourself and your project, you should be ready to ask these questions:

- What types of books have you edited (fiction, nonfiction, etc.)?
- What is your writing and editing background?
- What are your major editing accomplishments?
- What is unique about your editing process?
- What types of books do you enjoy working with?
- Are you willing to provide an editing sample?
- What makes you a good fit for my manuscript?
- Can you provide at least two references of books you've edited in the last two years that are close to my genre/subject matter?
- BONUS QUESTIONS – Ask him or her about the WORST project or book they've worked on, and why it went wrong.

Your next step: Interview the editor's past clients. This is probably the most important step of all. Regardless of how you developed your shortlist of authors, be sure to talk to someone the editor has worked with in the past. If any editor refuses to provide a reference – even if it's just a written recommendation from a client – drop them from consideration.

As you talk to a previous client of a prospective editor, ask these key questions:

- Were you happy with the quality of work?
- Did the editor communicate well with you?

- What was the format of the final product delivered?

- Did the editor meet the agreed-upon deadline?

- Did you end up paying what the editor quoted at the outset of the project?

- Did the editor have a positive attitude throughout the project?

- Does the editor live locally? If not, were you able to work electronically?

- Last and most important: Would you hire this editor again?

Consider the Costs

So how much is a good editing job gonna set you back? Let's use a fiction book of 100,000 words for our example. Proofreading is the least expensive option but will cost in the high hundreds of dollars. A typical line editor charges about $25 to $50 per hour, depending on their level of experience and expertise and on the subject matter, and they generally complete five to ten pages an hour. Engaging even a $25-per-hour copy editor for a 75,000-word novel will cost you about a thousand dollars. Substantive editing is likely to put you back $50 or more per hour, and the typical working rate is several pages per hour.

Doing a sample quote with my friends at FirstEditing.com reveals this price quote of our sample fiction book with a word count of 75,000 words:

PRICE	DELIVERY
$1065	10-14 Days Standard Service
$1438	Rush B Service with 9-10 Days Delivery
$1864	Rush A Service with 7-8 Days Delivery

With many editors you can negotiate to pay by the hour, by the project (a flat fee), or by the page. Most reputable editors work with an hourly rate, which is the most effective and allows the editor to do their best work. You can, of course, specify a cap on how many hours the editor is allowed to bill for. Some editors may ask for a percentage of the total payment up front or after you receive a specified proportion of the edited material.

Is it really worth it?

In a word: Yes. This is an area a lot of self-published authors have chosen to short change, and it's cost them. Consider the return on investment: If you choose to go the traditional publishing route, a literary agent will be impressed with your tight, cleanly written prose. If you're going direct and publishing yourself, the requirements for editing are just as strict. In fact it's even more vital for you to have a set – or sets – of other eyes on your prose before it hits the marketplace because your writing reputation is on the line. No subject matter or genre is exempt from this requirement.

It's nearly impossible to quantify the effect of an editorial professional's contribution to the impact of any content, and in many cases, the editing you don't notice is the best kind. In a sense, it's a leap of faith to hire an editor. There's no guarantee that employing an editor (even one armed with an impressive resume or glowing testimonials) will result in huge sales when it finally hits the stores. But if you're careful, you'll inevitably reap the benefits of better quality content.

If your book requires extensive line editing, then our six-week timetable might not be possible. Just like our cost rationale, the time spent to improve your book is a sound investment.

So what if your editing budget is exactly $0?

I get it. You might not have the budget for nor the goals that mandate the use of a professional editor. But that doesn't mean you need to completely rely on your own self editing before launching your book into the marketplace. There are actually some pretty decent automated online editing resources that can possibly improve your book and that won't break the bank:

If you've got a small budget, you might be interested in:

- AutoCrit Editing Wizard. (https://www.autocrit.com/editing/free-wizard/)You can try out the non-member's demo with a 500 word sample and view the various reports, including overused words, sentence variation, clichés & redundancies and many more. Non-paying authors can only submit 500 words per day. If you want to upgrade, there are 3 memberships: Gold (1,000 words for $47), Platinum (8,000 words for $77) and Professional (100,000 words for $117).

- EditMinion (http://editminion.com/) is a useful program, as it highlights weak words, adverbs, sentences ending in prepositions and a passive voice. Free users can only submit a small writing sample but it could point out problems throughout your manuscript.

- Pro Writing Aid (http://prowritingaid.com/)is a free editing software that catches things like sticky sentences (sentences with too many glue words), vague and abstract words, overused words, repeated words and phrases, complex words and pacing. It also offers a premium paid version that's packed with a lot of editing tools for just $35 per year.

Editing can be fun. Yes, really.

If you want to take a break from what can be a mind-numbing part of the process, here are some good time wasters:

- Ever wonder if you're writing is subconsciously influenced by Steven King or Patricia Cornwell? Click over to I Write Like (http://iwl.me/) and paste your text in the designated box. This fun tool will examine your writing style and choice of words and then compare the sample to works penned by famous writers throughout the ages.

- The Hemingway App is both fun and useful http://www.hemingwayapp.com/). Papa always cut straight to the chase without a lot of wasted verbiage. Follow the instructions on the site and paste your text in. For sentences highlighted in yellow, you're advised to split or shorten it to make it clearer. The red highlight indicates the sentence is extremely dense or complicated, and you'll likely lose your reader's attention.

- The Writer's Diet (www.writersdiet.com) is much the same as the Hemingway App, with fewer cats. This feedback tool helps you slim down your writing to the bare minimum. This automated tool will suggest which words and phrases you should lose to improve your writing.

Whether you choose to pay for your self-editing software or use a free version, remember that a program cannot replace a human being.

Is it really worth it? Take 2

So don't take just my opinion for it. A recent Writer's Digest survey amongst self-published authors illustrates the value of editing.

The chart below illustrates the two-year earnings of books produced by indie authors and the percentage of those who chose to use an editor:

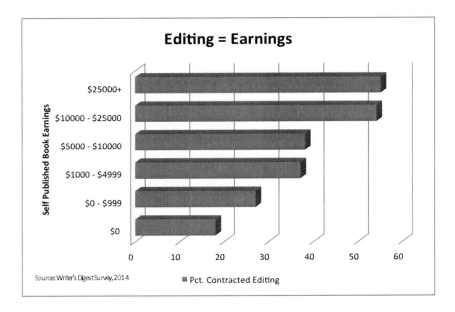

This study suggests there's a strong correlation between authors who see the wisdom of professional editors and strong book sales. There's a similar trend with cover design services, as we'll soon learn.

Partnering with your editor

No one really likes to be edited. Including me. But you have to realize the editor's role in the process. Remember first that your editor is not your high school English teacher who lives to drill in some arcane writing rule. The vast majority of editors know how to interact with authors in a respectful, professional relationship. They have to make a living, and they would quickly find themselves unable to if they went out of their way to hurt authors' feelings or insult them. They also have a reputation to uphold, and it's important they produce great value for their clients. Throughout history, authors have relied on their editors to be their sounding boards, to represent the eye and ear of the reader, and to bring a viewpoint that can't arise spontaneously in the author's head. We may live in an age where more people are staring at glowing characters on a screen than paper and ink, but nothing has really changed.

More important, though, the point at which you engage an editor is the point at which you take off your author hat and put on your product developer hat. You and your editor are a team, trying to put out the best product you can, so that it will be embraced by your target audience.

Step 3 – Pick your publishing path.

Laying out all the options for your writing career

TIMELINE: 1 WEEK

My dream has always been to reach a lot of readers, and make a living doing something I love.

-J.A. Konrath, self-published author who has sold hundreds of thousands self-published books through Amazon. His blog is a must read -http://jakonrath.blogspot.com/

When our good friends and BookBaby partners over at Amazon launched the Kindle, I don't think even Jeff Bezos himself foresaw the self-publishing revolution that continues to sweep the globe. As the technology has matured and stabilized, it's even more obvious how the publishing world has flipped around to give authors all the leverage. Simply put, there's never been a better time in recorded history to be a writer. Your options are many; your opportunities are vast!

While your book is being edited, the first decision you need to make is what you'll do with your freshly edited manuscript. It's a big choice – almost as big as the one you made when you decided to first put pen to paper, or keystrokes to the screen, and write that book. To help you make up your mind, we'll cover all the options in this chapter as we:

- Outline and explain the two basic publishing options now available to writers everywhere.

- Examine the pros and cons of traditional publishing, where authors enjoy marketing and distribution support. But it comes at a price – both monetary and creative control.

- Explore the still-emerging world of self-publishing, where authors are their own boss. Plus they're the marketer, salesperson and every other job along the publishing pathway.

The publishing crossroads

Every so often you read about so-and-so signing a contract for a lucrative book deal. Six figure advances, press junkets, book tours and all the trimmings of a big-time publishing deal. Unless you happen to be an ex-President writing his memoirs, or a naughty celebrity penning a tell-all book, don't expect this kind of treatment. I'm sure that's not news to anyone reading this book. Still, every writer has options for how his or her manuscript can reach the marketplace. But now their journey needs to be angled in one direction or the other, like a T in the road.

You have two basic options:

1. Pursue the time-honored traditional publishing path. This involves finding an agent to help edit and represent your work, submitting your book to publishers large and small, and putting your book in the hands of industry experts for all marketing and sales activities.

2. Or you can go the self-publishing route, either completely DIY or with the assistance of digital publishing converters/distributors (like BookBaby). You're in control, with a choice of selling printed books

or eBooks – or both – directly through Amazon, Barnes & Noble and many other portals (including your own).

In truth, there is a third option that we'll explore more at the end of the book. But for now we'll stay with these two channels. Both of these routes are crowded with authors who've found fame and fortune and many more who have found neither. Let's help you make your best decision by considering the pros and cons of each route.

Traditional Publishing Pros

For the very privileged few authors with "star power" or celebrity appeal, the traditional publishers offer a very attractive option. But you don't necessarily have to be a Kardashian to have a chance to be chosen for this channel, and there are some tangible benefits to going down this road. Here is a list of the "pros" to snagging that publishing deal:

Creative services with all the trimmings – It starts with editing. How can the manuscript realize its full potential? Are there problems to fix? Polishing needed? At a publisher, the "development editor" is assigned manuscripts as they are acquired and is responsible for getting them into shape (at children's publishers, the acquisition and development editor are usually the same person). Next it needs a copyeditor's eagle eye to check for correct spelling, grammar, and punctuation; to create a consistent approach to such things as compound words; to do some light fact-checking; and perhaps to mark up titles, heads, and subheads.

So much for the words – how about the look of your book? What's so complicated about designing a book? Anyone can do it with a word processor, right? Well, not if you want a book that's optimally designed for ease of reading, with a typeface that suits your subject, and that doesn't just look like every other book on the market. And then there is the jacket, to make the book stand out. Publishers keep designers on staff, or hire freelancers. In the traditional publishing model, books go through several rounds of revisions as part of the deal.

As a rule, it's fair to say that publishers know better than authors what cover or title a book needs.

For those who have chosen to be part of the publishing process, manuscripts and their authors must successfully run the publishing gauntlet – literary agencies, acquisitions editors, contractual negotiations, editing, production, and marketing. It's safe to say that many books go through this process with publishing professionals – people who more often than not know a good book when they see one. Manuscripts that get through a publisher's rigorous screening process are more likely to emerge as worthwhile, readable books.

Marketing Muscle – This area is one of the biggest "pros" of having a traditional book deal. Marketing is half the work of selling books – the other half is writing them. Publishing houses' book marketing department s work to get an author's book in front of bookstore buyers and book distributors, in order to make sure your book is available (and, hopefully, displayed) to the consumer public. As the number of bookstores decline, they're now focusing more on other outlets once dismissed as too small or unimportant. These can include specialty accounts, libraries and gift shops. Online retailers are now probably the most important channel, and they work for special placements and advertising support on the Internet.

In traditional publishing, each book is assigned a marketer who is usually working on dozens of titles at any one time. The most important part of this person's job involves the marketing strategy for the book. The marketer determines the potential readers for an individual book, the size of the market for the book, and a strategy for how best to reach the readers who might be interested in the book.

The marketing department's main job is getting the word out about your book. While print advertising has waned, it still exists in vehicles like The New York Times Book Review. Online ads are increasingly more common. The marketing department and a book's marketing budget determines if, where and when a book will be advertised.

Marketers are also tasked with reaching out through social media and to key bloggers. These blogging tastemakers are an important part of getting buzz in the marketplace.

Distribution – If you want to get your book into bricks-and-mortar bookstores, it's a lot harder when you self-publish. Traditional publishers already have a print-and-distribution system in place, so they'll make sure your book is available wherever books are sold, online and offline. But if you self-publish, your books will primarily be available in the online space, which limits potential sales. Some self-published authors have successfully gotten their books into physical bookstores, but it requires a lot of legwork.

Having traditional distribution means you benefit from preorders, management of your book inventory, and having a sales force that's getting your book out to retailers on your behalf.

Some authors might want to dismiss the value of traditional store distribution. With the demise of chains like Borders (and Barnes and Noble is teetering on the brink as I type this) the popularly held belief is that the bookstore is nearly dead. And surely these retail outlets had a rough go of things in the early 2000s. About a thousand small and independent stores closed their doors. Yes, it seems that Amazon and the eBook have put the last nail in the coffin of the neighborhood bookstore. Except that's not true. According to the American Booksellers Association, since 2009 the number of bookstores has actually gone up, from 1,404 to 1,567. That's a small increase, mind you, but an increase nonetheless.

Independent bookstores currently sell 10% of the books, with Barnes and Noble selling 20%, and Amazon 29% (the remaining 40% of sales are spread thinly through 10 or so other outlets, from Target and Wal-Mart to audiobooks). The independent booksellers holding their share of the market are finding novel ways of staying relevant to their communities. And traditional publishers still hold the key to getting books into these venues.

The dream of every author: The advance check – Many traditional publishers offer authors an advance payment on their work. Once you are established as a recognized and saleable author, this could be a considerable amount. The advance awarded is against future sales, also called royalties. That is, publishers "advance" the author an amount of money based on what they think the book will earn. The amount of the advance against royalties is based on many factors: the size of the publisher, the historic performance of similar books in the marketplace and most especially the author's track record of previous book sales. The amount of a book advance can range from a thousand dollars for a new author at a small publisher to tens of millions of dollars for a bestselling author with a huge fan base. As the book goes on sale, the advance is then "earned out" when the author royalties from its sales surpass the advance that the publisher paid the author.

(Side note: Do you think you could turn down a seven-figure advance check? One author did – and couldn't be happier. More about him at the end of the book.)

Validation - Even though they don't always get it right, agents and publishers make a living choosing books that they think readers will embrace. Their job is to find the good stuff and get it to market. So traditionally published books do still have that extra stamp of validation and credibility. The question is: Does the average reader check to see who published a book before they buy it?

There's also an ego-boosting component to this channel that can't be denied. It's a goal of millions of would-be authors to sign that publishing deal. I talk to authors every week that still state this as their primary publishing goal.

Traditional Publishing Cons

And now a few reasons the legacy publishing model may not be for you:

Loss of Creative Control – When you go with a traditional publisher, they gain rights to your book. And that means all creative elements to your work. Those words you spent hours, days, weeks – even years – working on are now pretty much the property of your publisher. Some authors might be fine with that. After all, these are the so-called publishing experts who have shaped the literary world for the past few hundred years. You're in good hands, right? Right?

Contracts vary but as an example, they're going to decide what cover and title go on your book. You might have no say over what's on the book covers or even the title of the book. The idea of the book that you have poured your soul into being drastically altered by an editor is utterly heart-wrenching to many writers.

Giving up distribution rights – Again, contracts will vary, but often publishers also own printing and distribution rights for a specified amount of time. At conferences I speak with authors who are counting down the days until they regain control of their book rights. And I'm not talking about famous writers; these are the folks who wrote books 10 or even 20 years ago – well before the words "digital publishing" were even known. Some of them represent estates of deceased authors with substantial backlists. They're still the contractual property of publishing houses, most of whom have no interest or inclination to rerelease any of the titles. These all-inclusive publishing contracts were written in such a way as to allow the publishers to assume any and all unspecified rights – and eBooks fell under this clause.

The true cost of traditional – Agents and publishers cost a lot of money. Everyone gets a cut – the editors, proofreaders, cover designers, layout designers, distributors, etc… The list goes on and on. You're sharing profits with everyone involved in producing your book, so you get a much smaller royalty. An average advance these days could be as low as $5000 and royalties are about 7-10% for a paperback and 25% for an eBook.

But it goes much farther than that. Publishers take the lion's share of royalties, usually 85-92%. That means most authors earn about a buck per book, or less. Publishers hog roughly 70% of electronic royalties, for a product that has almost no production or distribution costs.

Marketing reality – The description above about traditional publishing's marketing muscle is true – but only for a few authors with a strong selling track record. For most new authors, publishers don't do a lot of marketing. You're lucky if they send you on a book tour. Many traditionally published authors hire their own PR firms and marketing professionals and pay for these costs out of pocket. Again, this can vary depending on your contract, but unless you have what they think is going to be a blockbuster (or if you're already hugely successful), traditional publishers don't usually invest a whole lot in marketing a new author.

Timeliness – We've already talked about how the traditional publishing path is long and time-consuming. But it's a huge consideration, so let's review it again: After you finish writing your book, it can take months to get an agent (if you get one at all), and then it can take many more months to sell it to a publisher (if you sell it at all). From there, it's usually about a year before the book hits stores. I'd say most authors wait 1-2 years (minimum) between finishing their book to seeing it in stores—and that's if everything moves along on schedule. Some of that time is useful; you can start working on your next book and you can get your marketing plan going. Some authors don't mind but others are frustrated, especially when that 1-2 years turns into 3-4 years or more.

Here's another take on the timeliness issue. Almost all traditional publishers issue royalty statements every six months. This means that authors are paid only twice a year –- and then only if their advances have earned out and there are thus royalties owing to them. Even if their advances have earned out, authors still never know how much money, if any, they will receive during any given pay period. This is because, usually, until receipt of their royalty statements, they never know how many books they have actually sold, or what reserve against returns is being held by the publisher for that pay period.

What is a reserve against returns? Unlike most merchandise, creative works like books and CDs are sold on a returnable basis. That means that if a retail bookstore orders 100 copies of an author's book and doesn't sell any of them, then the bookstore can return all 100 copies to the publisher, for credit --which the publisher then charges back against the author's royalties, as well. (Mass-market paperback books have only their covers stripped and returned, while the books themselves are required to be destroyed. Sales of these stripped books are illegal.)

In order to avoid overpaying the author, the publisher will therefore withhold a percentage of the author's royalties against returns. If, for instance, unsold books are being returned to the publisher at a rate of 50% -- meaning that out of 100,000 books shipped to retail bookstores and wholesalers (who also stock outlets such as supermarkets), 50,000 books have already been returned unsold, then the publisher may withhold 50% of the author's royalties, as a reserve against returns.

Timeliness, take 2 – You need to show almost instant sales results. If your book doesn't succeed during the publisher's time frame (usually the first year — or less), you are labeled a failure. It's possible you'll get one more chance, but the truth is, you're tarnished goods in that model. If you are lucky enough to get a second deal, but it doesn't perform in the publisher's allotted time, then you're probably finished with that publisher. They simply can't afford to be patient. Publishers are constantly releasing other books, working publicity schedules and vying for shelf space at bookstores. The deadlines for being considered a success have nothing to do with your particular book. They have everything to do with the amount of time your ADD publisher is willing to spend with your book before moving on to the next thing the company is publishing.

The odds are not in your favor – As you probably already know, traditional publishing is very hard to break into. How hard? J.K. Rowling's first Harry Potter book was rejected by a dozen publishers. *A Time to Kill*, bestselling author John Grisham's first novel, was rejected by 16 agents, then a dozen publishers. Publishers today are spending most of their energy and cash on "front-list" books — their new books that stand a chance of becoming bestsellers. Other types of books, no matter how worthy they and their authors may be, are finding fewer and fewer opportunities with major publishers. These are "midlist" books —information books, how-to books, cookbooks, regional history books, first novels. Indeed, some publishers are increasingly ceding this ground to regional publishers, print-on-demand publishers, and the group we'll explore next – self-publishers.

Self-publishing – power to the author

It's well known that self-publishing is the fastest growing segment of the publishing industry, fueled by the rapid growth in popularity of eBooks and digital reader devices. Just like their musical brethren who bypass the big record labels and distribute music directly to their fans, authors can now go direct to readers by publishing eBooks for Kindles, iPads and Nooks.

Beyond the exploding sales numbers, the electronic publishing age offers opportunities for new and prospective authors that have previously been open to a relative few.

The odds are very much in your favor. Thousands of manuscripts are submitted to agents and publishers every year; only a handful are accepted. I'd say most authors are still holding on to "The Dream". You know the one – how your manuscript is that one in a million slam dunk best seller that's going to capture an agent's eye out of the hundreds or thousands he or she receives each year. So it's time to get real. One industry source I've seen says your odds of finding an agent and then a publisher are perhaps 0.01%. Compare that with your chances of getting your book self-published – 100%.

Authors in control – With eBooks, authors can finally have as much control as they want because of their direct access to their reading audience. Every self-published author I've spoken with while writing this book cited creative control as one of the main reasons they chose to self-publish. They want control over the production aspects of their book. They decide what their book will look like, how much it will cost, what formats it will be available in, and more. They want creative control over future editions, eBooks, audio books, marketing, and public relations. They want foreign publishing and, yes, even the movie rights.

Most self-publishing options will not involve you signing any long-term contracts. As such, you have the option of taking your book or other material somewhere else. You can always decide to try traditional publishing if you aren't happy with self-publishing or if your needs exceed what self-publishing can handle.

Weeks not months – In the "publisher in control" model, when an author finally completes his or her manuscript, it's a classic case of hurry-up-and-wait. It can take anywhere from 12 to 18 months for the traditional author-agent-publisher-designer-printer-bookstore model to get the work into the marketplace. Compare that with the approximately six weeks it takes to see your book on Amazon, Apple and more when you self-publish. Think of it – if you choose to self-publish you could be writing your fourth or fifth book before your first traditionally published volume makes its way to the bookstores. We all know the saying about how "life is short." It's too short to wait on a publisher.

Longer shelf life – In traditional publishing, your book is usually given a one big marketing push. If it doesn't sell well in that season, you're pretty much finished, and your book will go on the publisher's mid- or backlist. Self-publishing allows you the benefit of long-tail marketing, meaning you can promote your book for years at your own level of comfort, effort, and speed, as finances and time permit, and using methods that make the most sense for you. In the world of self-publishing, you have time on your side. You can have a book that doesn't sell well, and then you can write another book. If that doesn't sell perfectly, guess what? You can write another book. That doesn't mean I'm advocating that authors choosing to self-publish should just upload pure garbage to Amazon and hope people will actually pay money for it. I'm suggesting that a book not selling might be about visibility rather than writing talent. Sometimes it takes time to for a book to be seen and gain traction. And truth be told, it also requires luck. The more books you publish, the more likely you are to increase your chances of gaining traction and getting lucky.

Develop your own niche – Your book doesn't have to be about vampires, 50 shades of whips and chains, or the latest social meme to be published. Traditional publishers are looking for novels that either fit a formula or easily defined niche. If it takes more than 30 seconds to explain to an agent or publisher what your book is about…you're never going to get their attention. It's not that way with readers, however. Consumers get tired very quickly of the same-old, same-old formula. How many vampire stories do you really want to read? With some of the marketing tools mentioned in the upcoming chapter you can find your niche audience.

Money in the bank – While self-publishing advocates told me that control was an important component to their decision, it was easily topped by the authors' interest in realizing real financial gains. Not every self-published book is guaranteed to sell, of course. But those that do reward self-published authors in ways that traditional publishing houses cannot match.

How is it that authors are making more per copy from $2.99 eBooks than traditionally published authors are with $10.99 eBooks? Does it mean everyone should self-publish?

First, some important background information to start:

Standard royalties via traditional publishers (note: these may vary):
Hardcover: 10% retail, sometimes escalating to 15% after sales thresholds are met
Trade paperback: 7.5% retail
Mass market: 8% retail
EBook: 25% net (usually translates to 17.5% retail)

Kindle revenue share for self-published authors
Priced higher than $9.99: 35% retail

Priced between $2.99-$9.99: 70% retail

Priced below $2.99: 35% retail

B&N revenue share for self-published authors

Priced higher than $9.99: 40% retail

Priced between $2.99-$9.99: 65% retail

Priced below $2.99: 40% retail

Approximate eBook market share

Amazon: ~55%

B&N: ~25%

Others (Kobo, Apple, Google, Sony, etc.): ~20% combined

On average, traditional publishers pay royalties of between 7.5% and 12% of the book's cover price. If your book sells for $19.99, that means you might get about $1 to $2.40 per book in royalties.

The old payment formulas are completely upside down in the self-publishing eBook world. Instead of accepting miniscule royalty percentages going through old school publishers, authors are seeing up to 70% of sales receipts through some of the online retailers. Even when eBook authors bring prices way down to 2.99....$1.99....even $.99...they're realizing much higher revenue totals because of increased unit sales.

Let's explain this using a scenario. Let's say you've hit the publishing lottery, found an agent and publisher. An author signing a first contract can expect to receive an advance of anywhere from $1,000 to $10,000, on average, per book. Naturally, there are exceptions to this rule. However, it would be unwise and unrealistic with regard to your financial planning to assume you will be that rare, unknown author who garners a multimillion-dollar advance. So let us say the author receives a $10,000 advance for a single book. That means the author would subsequently need to earn $10,000 in royalties from the sales of that book before receiving any additional income from it.

If the author did not subsequently earn at least $10,000 in royalties from the sales of the book, then the contract would be unearned, and no additional royalties would ever be paid to the author. Further, the publisher might well -- depending upon the terms of the contract -- also have the right to demand the return of that portion of the advance that was unearned. For example, if the author's royalties amounted to a grand total of only $3,000, then the publisher could request that the remaining unearned $7,000 of the advance be repaid to it by the author (although this rarely ever happens in practice).

Generally speaking, hardcover books pay standard royalty rates of 10% on the first one to 250,000 copies sold. The percentages usually go up on a sliding scale on high scales but let's not consider that for this example. So if an author's hardcover book has a cover price of $25.00, then the author will earn only a $2.50 royalty on every copy sold, up to 250,000 copies.

This means that if only 10,000 copies of the author's book are ever sold, then the author will earn only $25,000. This sum may indeed be fairly lucrative if the book took only a short time to write. However, if the author spent several years writing the book, then obviously, it was not very financially productive.

You would think the standard royalty rates for hardcover books would also be the same for mass-market paperback books, since because the cover prices for paperbacks are much lower, the royalty rates would be comparably much lower, too. However, this is, in fact, not the case.

Generally speaking, the standard royalty rates for paperback books vary from a low of 1% to a high of 10%, with the average royalty rate falling at 6%. So if an author's paperback book has a cover price of $6.50, then at a 6% royalty rate, the author will earn only a $.39 royalty on every copy sold. This means that if only 10,000 copies of the author's book are ever sold, then the author will earn only $3,900.

Now let's take those same 10,000 books sold, but this time we'll assume that you've self-published this as an eBook. Let's further assume you've put the book on sale at the currently popular retail price of $4.99. It's quite likely that an author selling 10,000 hardcover books at $24.95 would sell many more of the same title at $4.99 online but we'll assume the worst case scenario.

If they all sold through Amazon, the numbers would look like this:

10,000 books sold

Total sales @$4.99 each – $49,900.

Net sales revenue (70%) – $34,930

It doesn't take a math whiz to understand how there is no question that self-publishing presents a much more lucrative opportunity for most authors.

The downside of DIY

Self-publishing isn't for everyone for a variety of reasons.

Upfront investment – While there are some absolutely free options available for self-publishing, the vast majority of authors will need help in getting their book to the marketplace, starting with editing and cover design and going all the way to optional marketing and printing costs if you choose the analog route as well. How much depends upon some formula that considers your hopes, dreams, aspirations…and disposable income. On average most self-published authors spend over $1000 before their book has made its first sale on Amazon.

Control is a double-edged sword – Remember how happy you were about having complete creative and financial control of your book? It's a wonderful thing, and it comes with a heavy burden of responsibility on the author's shoulders. They have to manage every facet of their book production, or hire it out. The time it takes to search, vet, interview and hire your "team" is considerable.

Put on the marketer's hat – I did a talk a couple of years ago at the Philadelphia Writer's Conference titled "Think Like A Marketer". The talk centered on how authors have to put down the 'pen' (wow, that dates me) and pick up the marketer's hat. I talked about how they need to look at their book as if it's a basic product, or even an ordinary commodity. In my PowerPoint presentation, I showed pictures of books opposite such basic staples of life as dog food, laundry soap and toilet paper. I looked out at the audience during this slide and saw a lot of shocked and sad faces. Surprisingly, I was not invited back to speak again. Most authors don't like to do book marketing. Those who self-publish understand it's a necessary evil. Some of the more successful ones do their homework, put in the hours it takes to promote their product and enjoy the results.

No room on the bookshelf. It's almost impossible for self-published authors to get distribution in a bricks-and-mortar store like Barnes & Noble. Don't take it personally – it's not that you're a bad author or that your book isn't any good. It's all about risk. Book distribution is the main dividing line between self-publishing and publishing with a traditional publisher. In fact, it's really the main argument for publishing with a traditional press. As the publishing business gets even more difficult, even small traditional presses cannot get into major chains, or even small independents, so self-published novels are even a further step behind. While people are increasingly buying books online, having a book in a bricks-and-mortar store is a great advertisement: A customer may buy a book online but only after checking it out in person in store.

The main reason that bookstores won't carry self-published books is because of the store's potential to take a loss on the book. Bookstores need the assurance that a publisher will buy back unsold books and this is not the case with most self-published authors. Because self-published books are less likely to sell, due to less marketing muscle, most bookstores just aren't willing to take the chance. Your best opportunity might be through local or regional stores that feature area authors. Depending on your book's genre or subject matter, there might be other opportunities as well.

Either, Or...or Both

There's a lot to consider between traditional and self-publishing. Authors everywhere should rejoice at having such a choice. There was a time when self-publishing was a last resort, a final attempt after an author had accumulated piles of rejections. Back then it was called working with a "vanity press", where authors bankrolled their own literary dreams with little hope of ever recouping their investment. While those same publishing scams continue to this day, the rapid pace of technology has made self-publishing easy and accessible. As a result, millions of authors have elected to self-publish without even bothering with traditional publishing.

The stigma of self-publishing has faded but many authors still diligently query agents and publishers, hoping to get their books published by traditional means. The good news is that now authors have a choice. It's no longer a matter of choosing the better option but choosing the option that is right for you. More and more authors are choosing to self-publish, even when they may have an interested publisher. In turn, as authors gain knowledge and awareness of the steps involved (including professional editing, of course), the quality of self-published books improves, lending further credibility to self-publishing in general.

Self-publishing has opened the gates, and it's true that a lot of low quality books have hit the market—poorly written manuscripts packed with typos and just plain bad storytelling, with awful covers to boot. But readers are smart. They know how to read the first few pages, check the reviews, and filter the good stuff from the bad stuff.

However, we used to think the guardians of the traditional publishing were pretty smart too. Up until a couple of years ago, agents and publishers acted as gatekeepers. They and they alone decided whose books got published. People – especially publishing industry folks - said they prevented bad writing from hitting the market. So why was Anne Frank's diary was rejected sixteen times? How could *Harry Potter and the Philosopher's Stone* be rejected eight times?

Chicken Soup for the Soul was rejected by over 100 publishers before its authors went ahead and published it themselves.

Obviously the acquisitions editors who passed on these and many other great books are not infallible. Conversely, there are a great many traditionally published books that are pretty bad in my humble opinion. What it comes down to is this: Your book can get rejected because whoever read it that day was in a bad mood, didn't like one of the characters, just read a similar story, or simply didn't care for the tone, style, or voice.

Do you really want to risk your literary career on the whims of an editor who had a fight with her husband?

This doesn't have to be an either/or kind of decision. Let me plant a seed right now that we'll discuss near the end of the book: The smart choice might be to do both. Set yourself up to self-publish your first book or books. Get out in the marketplace and experience the life of an author. You'll learn so much in the first six months after you've published that your second, third and following books will be that much better. Meanwhile an agent or publisher might find YOU and your traditional publishing career might just take off.

Step 4 – Crank up the book marketing machine.

Marketing is not an optional part of the process.

Almost anyone can be an author; the business is to collect money and fame from this state of being.
- A. A. Milne

Disclaimer: The topic at hand – book marketing – deserves far more than a chapter. Even a couple of chapters couldn't cover all there is to discuss about this important topic. There are a lot of books out there devoted to the subject. How many? As of the day I'm writing this, Amazon lists 11,295 titles under the search term "marketing for authors". There's no shortage of information out there about book marketing. Information overload is a real concern, especially for an author who doesn't like the now-necessary role of marketer.

We've allocated a week of your six-week sojourn to this topic, and that limited time period is wrong to the point of being false and misleading! Because once

The End. Now What? • 61

you've finished your book, the fact is that you need to be a marketer every single day, for as long as you're interested in making sales of your book.

What can you accomplish in the week we've allocated to this nearly lifelong endeavor? Enough to get your book marketing efforts machine up and running. In this portion of the book we'll:

- Take a first cut at the huge task of book marketing and divide it into two main categories.

- Focus mostly on the often overlooked areas of metadata and pricing. You might not finish the suggested activities in this time period but it's a solid start that can be completed at any time.

- Review a must-do marketing checklist for any author, plus a list of the best go-to marketing resources. Out of the thousands of blogs, websites and books, these are wellsprings of the best book marketing ideas that are worthy of your precious time.

Inside and Outside – the two book marketing categories

My approach to book marketing encompasses most of the usual elements. Unlike others, however, I first divide it into two major categories. Both are important and authors need to make sure they are taking care of both areas as they market.

In my marketing shorthand, I label these areas "Inside" and "Outside" but that's not descriptive enough. Perhaps the best way to illustrate my idea is for you to take on a different "persona" for a moment. Forget, temporarily, that you are an author. Instead, you are the owner of a small store. Let's say it's a gift store.

As a store owner, you have two main areas of concern in order to bring in sales:

1. You need to have an interesting yet well-organized store. It should be located in a good area so that people can find you. You must have

great inventory, first and foremost. It's better if you have a range of products but you can certainly start with one. You'll need great signage or sales staff that can provide all information to prospective buyers. It needs to be priced correctly, in line with your customers' expectations. In all, you're merchandising your store and making it very easy for people to buy.

2. And oh yes, people. That's the other thing you need: people, and lots of them. Even if you have meager sales goals, you'll need a large number of people viewing your store. Not all of them will buy; in fact, it will probably only be a fraction of them who actually make a purchase. How will you get people to come to your store? Through advertising, publicity–all kinds of promotional techniques.

Instead of using "inside" and "outside" to describe our categories, I prefer to use the terms bolded above.

Merchandising is mostly about presentation and positioning of a product within a store setting, be it a physical or an online place of commerce. In traditional retail commerce, visual display merchandising means merchandise sales using product design, selection, packaging, pricing, and displays that stimulate consumers to spend more. Many of these same concepts hold true for online marketing, although it's often less visual and more about descriptions. Authors can benefit by spending time studying these retailing techniques. In my opinion, most authors don't pay enough attention to these often overlooked opportunities.

Promotion is what most of those 11,000+ marketing books on Amazon deal with. From social media to email, websites to YouTube, authors have dozens of ways to push their books and attract readers. Some techniques work better than others, as a rule. But the old disclaimer, "Your results may vary", is very much at play. What works for one author or genre may very well not work for others. You can spend hours – and a lot of money – in this area without getting any return on your investment. And, sad to say, there are a lot of scammers in this space, promising unrealistic results in exchange for some of your hard-earned dollars.

How much can we accomplish in one week on your journey to the market-place? Quite a lot, actually, and without spending anything more than some focused hours of your time.

Setting up your "shop"

So here we are in your little retail store. What needs to be done?

First you need inventory. The more of it the better, and that especially goes for books. I don't mean to depress you on your first time out of the publishing gate, but your fifth book will probably be your best selling tool for your first book. Readers seem to be attracted to authors that have a lot to say. That's not to mean you can't sell your one and only book if that's what you have today. But just remember that your best marketing and sales techniques might be the amount of time spent writing.

Let's assume you do have multiple titles. People browsing your Amazon pages or – better still – your own website need to see how prolific you are. When you have ample inventory you can use the classic sales tool of sampling – giving your prospects a chapter or two of your current or upcoming book. And all good retailers know how to repackage items; in this case you could bundle multiple books together. Or maybe you've already serialized your work by sell-ing chapters as "singles". There are many ways you can use your own content for marketing.

Of course, your packaging needs to be eye-catching. We'll devote an entire chapter to the importance of cover design, so we'll skip it here.

How about your in-store signage? For the author advertising on the Internet, I equate this concept to the all-important metadata that is a constant compan-ion to every eBook.

Data about Data

Metadata — the word itself sounds so cold and robotic, like a character from a new Star Trek movie. Actually, it's one of the least-known and -understood components to publishing an eBook, but it's critical to your marketing and sales efforts.

Metadata is all the information related to a specific book — from the title, author name, and ISBN all the way through the synopsis, marketing copy, author bio, and cover images. To put it another way, metadata is the who, what, when, and where of your eBook. When your eBook is listed on an online store, customers will see an image of your cover which they can click on for more information about your work and to access the actual content of your work.

During the process of uploading your book – either directly to, say, Amazon or through a company like BookBaby - you'll be prompted to provide information about your book that will include:

- Author biography.
- The genre and subgenre of your book, so it can be categorized correctly in eBook stores.
- Short and long book descriptions that will be listed on your book pages on our partners' stores.
- Keywords that will aid readers searching for your book on Amazon.

Different online retailers ask self-published authors to provide metadata in slightly different amounts, in slightly different formats, and in different orders. But they ask for the information either in online forms or in formatted spreadsheets, so all you have to do is fill in the blanks. There are other items, but these are the most critical elements. What's so important about metadata? Browsing through the online bookshelves usually begins with a search. If your metadata does not reflect what someone is searching for, no one will ever find your book. It doesn't matter if you have an eye-catching cover or an attention-grabbing title. It doesn't matter if your prose is sheer perfection. Without good information about your book, you'll be confined to the virtual back shelves in our modern bookstores.

Here's a good quick start video to get you started: http://authormarketingclub.com/members/demo-amazon-description-generator/

So how do you go about creating good metadata? I've picked up some ideas talking to some of the most successful authors on BookBaby and came up with a few twists of my own. Get out a pad of paper or open up a spreadsheet program – this is going to take some research time to do it right. This is where you should spend most of your allotted week:

Start by going to Amazon.com, Apple's iBooks or BN.com and look up books like yours. What categories are they in? Study the book descriptions. See what words they've used to describe their books. Write down the ones that appeal to you. Now think about your own book. Jot down a list of words associated with the subject and genre of your book.

Next we head to the company that I like to call God's gift to marketers. That would be Google, and the Adwords Keyword Planner (https://adwords.google.com/KeywordPlanner). It's a tremendous window into what people are searching for through Google. To use it you'll need to sign in using a Gmail account or create one. Don't worry – this is completely free. You won't have to spend a dime.

Next, enter all of the keywords and phrases you listed out before. This way you can determine how often they are being searched, and whether the competition for these keywords is high, medium, or low.

I advise you to keep a spreadsheet with all of your results. It can get very complex and it will be valuable for you to have this incredible information at your fingertips. Once you've loaded these words in, you can see what combinations might work best for your book. The goal is very simple: You want to find phrases and word combinations with high search counts. But you also want the words that list medium to low competition. This combination gives you your best chance of coming near the top of the page on search results.

Next you put your newfound intelligence to work. Go back to Amazon and the search field. Start entering the words you've determined meet the criteria (high search/low competition). What you're hoping to find are words that auto-populate based on Amazon's own algorithms. Now Amazon doesn't publish their list of keywords. But when they pop up automatically, it is a dead giveaway that people – your potential readers - are using these terms to buy.

Some authors actually use this technique to come up with book titles. While this is an amazing scientific way to get maximum search potential on your book title, you'll need to make sure these different word combinations represent your book and its topic.

More on metadata

Genre plus – Your book can easily get lost in huge genre lists, so be as specific as you can be—the more precise the better. If you write "military history" your book will be competing with a lot of other books. The top spots in the query results list go to the highest-selling books. So if you're not already a best-selling self-published novelist, competing in a smaller arena gives your book a better chance at appearing on the customer's first page of results. To do this, modify the subject with a few focused words, from "military history" to "WW2 English aircraft comparison" or "RAF Spitfire versus Hurricane Hawker Pilots' Opinion", or whatever describes your book. Your book will have a better chance of standing out—and you'll attract the people who are seeking your specific niche.

Communicate the tone – Readers like to know the mood of your book. Readers often type in the feelings they want to take away from the experience of reading, so include those words in your metadata. List out all the adjectives that describe the emotions that your readers will feel when they read the books. Will they be on the edge of their seat in suspense? Will they be laughing? Will they wax nostalgic or become edgy? For this keyword, think about your readers' state of mind as they read, not the way how your characters feel in the book.

Beyond the topic – You can list out important and specific details of your book. For the WWII aircraft book above: Are pilots interviewed? How about aircraft mechanics? Those are potential keywords. Does the book discuss any locations or events? Put in words like "Battle of Britain", "London Blitz" and terms like that might be searched. Think about the other specific yet unique elements of your story—the city or country it's set in, the time period it takes place. Someone may be looking for those very qualities in a novel.

Reason to buy – Does your book make a great "Anniversary Gift" or "Graduation Present"? People going on vacation might use the term "Beach Reads" in their metadata. Customers seek books that fulfill their needs, so if your book can be used for a specific function, list it.

Play fair – One more tip. Don't try to game the system: Just don't. Don't mention other authors or titles in your metadata—even if everyone tells you your style is reminiscent of Ken Burns or Tom Clancy, do not put their names in your metadata. Online retailers police for cheats like that and they could de-list your book for it. Play fair—describe your book and your book only.

Authors are sometimes intimidated by the entire concept of metadata. If you use some of the ideas I've suggested, you can master it in no time. And if you don't succeed the first time – that's fine. You can go into your book listing and modify your metadata any time you like. While you can always tinker with the right words and phrases, pay heed to one more piece of advice. Always be consistent. Don't put one book description on Amazon and change it around for B&N. Use similar wording for the boilerplate on your press release, book flyer, etc. Create a document or spreadsheet documenting the metadata and where you used it. This is especially important if you have several titles and a huge time saver as you expand your marketing.

The price must be right

Our last merchandising task is pricing. Cruise any of the writer's forums on the Internet and you're bound to find a lot of discussions on the topic of eBook pricing.

You'll find legions of authors who are enjoying success — and best net sales revenue per book — at the currently popular price levels of $4.99 to $9.99. They're making the maximum royalty from the eBook retailers — up to 70% returned to the author — and believe the higher prices begin to reflect the quality and value of their efforts.

On the other side of the argument are hundreds of authors thrilled with the results of pricing their books down to rock bottom levels —99¢ to $1.99 — giving up the high percentage of return for larger numbers of fans. A few authors like John Locke have seen their literary fortunes soar with this pricing strategy.

Amazon's list of 100 best-selling books has become a pricing free-for-all. During the week I'm writing this, 28 books were selling for just 99¢. Others were priced at $4.98, $7.99, and more than a few at $9.99. The most expensive was Hillary Clinton's tome "Hard Choices" at $14.99. There is none of the clarity of iTunes in its early years, when the price of music tracks was fixed at 99¢.

Here's a chart compiled by Digital Book World that tracks the average price of the eBook bestsellers' list.

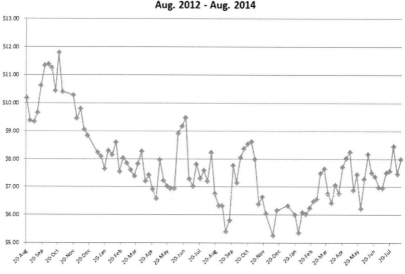

You'll note some price spikes during the pre-holiday months that are easily explained. What's interesting is the gradual rise in pricing in early and mid-2014. This coincides with the introduction of the Kindle First and Kindle Unlimited programs.

One of the biggest factors to consider in pricing your eBook is the percentage of sales you'll receive from the retailers. Amazon pays out a royalty of 70% on all Kindle titles priced between $2.99 and $9.99. For eBooks priced below $2.99 and above $9.99, Amazon pays out only 35%. Most of the other eBook retailers have similar price banding.

To encourage more readers with a low price and still get the 70% royalty, you would set your price to $2.99. Every sale will yield you a net royalty of $2.09 per sale.

If you opt to maximize your exposure and price your book at $0.99, then you'll get 35 cents per sale. In order to get $2.09 in royalties with a book priced at $0.99, you'll have to sell 6 books. If you sell 1,000 books at $2.99, then you'll make $2,090. If you are contemplating a price drop to $0.99, then you'll have to sell 5,972 books to make the same net royalties you did when it was priced at $2.99.

But writing and publishing an eBook is more than just numbers, dollars, and cents. These kinds of royalty calculations are only one factor in the success of an eBook. Why do some authors price their books at 99¢ when the math seems to be so against that model? Here are a few reasons:

It's only 99¢, what's the risk? – An impulse-priced book allows a reader take a chance on a book that looks interesting. If you're an unknown author trying to build your readership base, this might be the answer. While $3.99 doesn't sound like a lot, it does mean the difference between 1 book and 4 books for the purchaser.

An easier path to best-seller status – To rise atop the Amazon rankings is the Holy Grail quest for most every author. Amazon counts book sales units, not revenue. Setting your price at the impulse level of $0.99 could help you creep up in the ranking and gain visibility there — visibility you might not have gotten if you kept your book price higher.

Success begets success – When you visit your book page, you'll see a section that says "Customers Who Bought This Item Also Bought." The real value for you is when your book appears in that section on other successful books. Amazon will list up to 100 books in this section and readers will often scroll through that list to discover other books that look interesting. Again, a drop to 99¢ may be the catalyst to increase your sales enough to land you in that section on some popular books.

Those are a few of the arguments for dropping your Kindle book price to 99¢. Of course, pricing is only one factor in the success of a book. There's no guarantee your 99¢ book will attract hundreds of new readers — that's why it's important to continue to market your book and actively seek out ways to get it in front of new readers.

So what should you charge for your book? As the back-and-forth pricing arguments attest, there is no easy answer. It depends on your genre, your commitment to marketing, and the prevailing winds of the marketplace at any given time or place. New authors who are trying to find a readership can use the low price strategy to great success.

If you have a series, you may want to lower the first book in the series to entice people to give you a try. Other books can then be priced higher because you are no longer a new author to those who have purchased your book.

And if you're an established author finding success with eBooks, think long and hard about changing your book pricing strategy. If you are seeing success at one price, think hard before trying to cash in on a higher price. You don't want to kill the momentum of your sales; it may be a hard thing to restart if you do.

Like the rest of the eBook world, we're in a rapidly evolving environment when it comes to eBook pricing. Things are so new, and changing so quickly, that pricing strategies can be outdated in the blink of an eye. One of the great things for authors who self-publish their eBooks is the ability to change the price, test different price points, and react to the market demand.

Promotion basics

Our store is ready for business and we've put the big "OPEN" sign out front. Now we need to find readers. Lots of 'em.

So let's start with a very basic checklist of your must-have marketing to-dos:

- Author's blog – Do you have one? If yes, keep posting daily to maintain a lively and interesting blog that gets your audience to come to your site. If you don't have one, get started now.

- Other authors' blogs – Get involved with other authors now by providing those bloggers with content by guest blogging or commenting. When it's your time to promote, these folks will be glad to help.

- Facebook by genre – Facebook is a terrific place to interact with your audience if your genre is romance, children's fiction, or science fiction/fantasy.

- Goodreads – Owned by Amazon, and 25 million readers strong, you should get active in this community of readers now. Goodreads offers contests that draw new readers to your books.

- Promote on Pinterest – This site has grown to over 100 million users! Pull together great visuals that your audience finds intriguing and they may find your books intriguing, too.

- Twitter – There's power in 140 characters. If you have an account, provide valuable content for your audience—and keep your thumb on the pulse of what your audience is interested in, too.

- YouTube – Believe it or not, it's now the second-biggest search engine after Google. Find a way to get your content on YouTube. Maybe it's someone interviewing you. Maybe you've produced footage of yourself discussing your book or other topics. Better still would be videos of your panel appearances, talks, etc. It's yet another way to find new readers and engage with your following.

- Plan, plan, plan ahead – Start thinking about how you're going to launch the book. There are plenty of websites devoted to book launches and marketing. You can do promotions with email newsletters like Story Finds (www.storyfinds.com) and more.

All books can be GOOD sellers, if not BEST sellers. All books can find their niche audiences, if authors spend time planning and executing interactive book marketing strategies that truly engage with their audience. But that's a topic for another guide.

Marketing kickstart – Marketers like me know that authors like you don't enjoy marketing. And unfortunately that doesn't work in your favor. It means that there are thousands of websites, consultants, and companies offering marketing services, often at outrageous prices. The promises and guarantees they make are just as outrageous. So permit me to steer you in the direction of some of the best – and more reputable – organizations and companies available to help you promote your book:

Goodreads Giveaway – Authors who are members of Goodreads can choose to host giveaways. They can give away up to 10 copies of their book, but the book must be a physical copy (www.goodreads.com).

LibraryThing Member Giveaway – Sign up for LibraryThing (www.librarything.com/) and then set up an eBook giveaway. You can choose to give away up to 100 copies, as well as when and for how long the giveaway lasts. After the giveaway ends, LibraryThing sends you a list of the emails of everyone who won, and you can give them a copy of your eBook.

Noise Trade – Although Noise Trade started as a music marketing company, it has since expanded into eBooks and audiobooks. It is one of the BookPromo partners with BookBaby; authors sign up for free and can choose to either offer certain chapters or a whole book for free. In exchange for the book, readers provide their email address and zip code, helping to build the author's email list. Readers can also choose to tip the author, so in many cases even though the book is free, the author earns money (www.noisetrade.com).

Byliner – One of the new start-ups on the book promotion scene, the company sends out a weekly email highlighting eBooks and audiobooks to 1.2 million people (www.byliner.com).

Story Cartel – Another BookBaby BookPromo partner. You can offer your eBook free for a limited time on Story Cartel to attract new readers. This site is all about creating relationships with authors and readers and building lists. During a book's promotion, readers are able to download the book for free and are then encouraged to write a review. In exchange, the author gets a list of readers who download the book and can directly engage with them. Afterwards, readers can choose to be added to the author's newsletter (www. storycartel.com).

Wattpad – Wattpad is one of the largest sites where you can upload your work for free and get feedback. Wattpad is a direct connection between writers and 30 million readers, all over the world. Readers receive notifications whenever a new chapter of a story is posted. Many writers share their work serially, posting stories one chapter at a time, so readers keep coming back (www.wattpad.com).

Addicted to eBooks – To submit a link, sign up for an account. Books must be priced at under $5.99 and have at least 5 reviews on Amazon. There is also a separate section for books that are available for free, and the option to pay for ads on the site (www.addictedtoebooks.com).

AuthorBuzz – This marketing service has the potential to reach readers, bloggers, booksellers, and librarians. It's not free but it might be worth spending a little coin. The service works with five different sites: Shelf-Awareness.com, DearReader.com, BookMovement.com, PublishersMarketplace.com, and KindleNationDaily.com. As an author, you compose short notes to booksellers and librarians, readers and leaders of book clubs (when applicable). These can include any promotional information you choose, such as:

- Links to websites, blogs and excerpts
- Info on setting up phone chats or reading group visits
- Materials for newsletters
- Info about contests or giveaways
- Mentions of new reviews

The notes will be sent out, along with the book cover and in some cases an author photo, via the newsletters or websites. The notes will also be featured for one week on the AuthorBuzz.com website and archived indefinitely (www.authorbuzz.com).

Bargain Booksy – Another paid service but there's nothing like getting your book in front of serious readers who have opted in to receive book promotions. For $25-$50 (prices vary between genres) you get an email blast to 50,000 subscribers, a feature on Free Booksy and a feature on Bargain Booksy (www.bargainbooksy.com).

Book Sends – Book Sends is another daily email service, but with cheaper prices. The site says it has over 70,000 subscribers, with promotion prices ranging from $10 to $125, depending on the book's genre and price. In order for a book to be accepted for promotion, it must look professional (especially the cover), have at least 5 4/5-star reviews, and be full-length (www.book-sends.com).

BookDaily – This is another good site that acts as a tool in developing authors' online promotional strategies. A free BookDaily author account allows you to:

- Post the first chapter of any of your books for reader review
- Post your biography and photo
- Include a link to your website or your blog for new traffic and SEO value
- Load video about your book
- Receive a regular author marketing newsletter from thought leaders in digital book marketing
- Promote your work with our free widget, press release information, and more (www.bookdaily.com)

Kindle Books and Tips – For authors who have books on Amazon – and that should be all of them – this is a tremendous resource. They send out emails to subscribers and posts on the blog about book deals. The blog has been ranked the #1 blog in terms of paid subscriptions in the Amazon Kindle store since 2010 and is consistently ranked in the Top 100 for all Kindle titles – books, newspapers, and blogs combined – every day of the week, week in and week out (www.fkbooksandtips.com).

Story Finds – This book promotion site offers an interesting mix of offers for authors looking for economical promotion. It offers Free and Daily Specials (showcasing books on sale and books priced for $1 or less). But authors need to make a living and we understand that. That's why it highlights stories with varying price points in its Author Spotlight, 1st Chapter Spotlight and Themed Weeks. Story Finds also has a weekly book cover contest (www.storyfinds.com).

Bloggers who review

This can be a very powerful resource for authors just starting their writing career. I'll publish a list here but this is a part of the book that can fall out of date quickly. Start here and then use Google to find more.

Blog Nation – Here's the perfect place to start. It's a massive database of blogs of all kinds of interests, including book reviewers. As of this writing it lists over 1400 blogs that discuss new books. It has an RSS feature that allows you to constantly be exposed to new content and bloggers (www.blognation.com).

Blog Rank – This site is pretty much the same as Blog Nation except it ranks the sites using its own proprietary scoring system (www.blogmetrics.org).

Book Blogger Directory – This is another site that lists and categorizes book bloggers. It's a pretty comprehensive listing of bloggers' Book Blogs, separated by genre and listed alphabetically (http://bookbloggerdirectory.wordpress.com).

The Book Blogger List – And one more. I've included this one because it's a 100% opt-in list. Any blogger mentioned on this site has asked to be listed.

This database of book bloggers is organized by genre of interest. If a book blogger has expressed interest in multiple genres, they will be listed in each category (www.bookbloggerlist.com).

And finally

The Internet is fairly bursting at the electronic seams with blogs about writing and publishing. Some of them are great. And some are even better than that. The following list is the cream of the crop, the must-read blogs for every author:

Self-publishing

The BookBaby Blog (http://blog.bookbaby.com/)

The Newbie's Guide to Publishing (http://jakonrath.blogspot.com)

David Gaughran's blog (http://davidgaughran.wordpress.com/)

The Passive Voice (http://www.thepassivevoice.com/)

The Creative Penn (http://www.thecreativepenn.com/)

Self-publishing Team (http://selfpublishingteam.com/)

Writing

Write To Done (http://writetodone.com/)

The Write Practice (http://thewritepractice.com/)

Story Fix (http://storyfix.com/)

Lindsay Buroker's blog (http://www.lindsayburoker.com/)

Writer's Digest (writersdigest.com)

Marketing

Social Triggers (http://socialtriggers.com/)

Michael Hyatt's site (http://michaelhyatt.com/)

Copyblogger (www.copyblogger.com)

And of course Kindle Boards (http://www.kboards.com/) is a popular hang-out for self-publishers. It's a real mixture of those starting out and those that have already sold tens or hundreds of thousands of books – or are on their way there!

Step 5 – Cover Design: Don't try this at home.

Let visual experts design what is ultimately your most important marketing tool.

TIMELINE – 1 WEEK

The work never matches the dream of perfection the artist has to start with.
- William Faulkner

Books and their covers. Tempting as it might be, I'm going to avoid the cliché. You know the one.

And yet judge they will, those thousands of potential readers that size up the quality of your writing literally in the wink of an eye. The reality of the book industry is that the vast majority of readers do indeed use the cover of a book as a deciding factor in not only whether or not they should buy the book, but if they will enjoy it as well.

With millions of books for readers to choose from, the first "sales pitch" is the cover. If it is not striking enough to draw attention, it will be passed over for something more interesting on either side. And that's something you simply cannot afford to let happen as a new author.

In our 6-week timeline we've allotted just one week to come up with a great book cover. Is that enough time? Absolutely. As important as it is, this is an area where you shouldn't over-think it. If you focus on this for seven days with the design skills you already possess OR with the right cover artist, you'll have a winning design faster than you can imagine.

In this chapter our focus is on helping you create the ideal "packaging" for your well-chosen words as we:

- Reinforce the importance of your book cover and review some of the basics of good cover design.

- Discuss the pros and cons of hiring cover design professionals. You might find you can't afford NOT to have their help.

- Guide you through the process of vetting potential cover artists and suggest some good avenues to find cost-friendly designers on the Internet.

Dead giveaway

A well-designed cover is the first assurance the reader has that the book is of a high quality, both in content and delivery. Nobody would mistake me for having the most artistic eye and yet I can spot a 'home grown' cover a mile away. And so can you. When I see them, I usually think, *If the author didn't want to invest any time, effort of money on a decent cover design, I can only wonder at what shortcuts he took inside the book.*

Covers can scare away a customer or lure them in. Bad covers, with pixilated images, watermarks clearly visible, text badly formatted or aligned, or just plain ugly, suggest to the reader that the interior of the book will be equally sloppy.

And even if a poorly-conceived cover hasn't managed to discourage the reader, it's going to create preconceptions in their minds. With their attention already drawn to errors and sloppiness, they will more easily spot mistakes in the text, or might even go looking for them. Frankly, I'm a lot more forgiving of typos in what looks to be a professional work.

For the fortunate author who finds his work being published outside of the US, many recognize the need for different covers in different markets. Design principles vary across the globe. For instance, US covers often feature more detailed imagery, while UK covers will have far simpler designs with more frequent use of negative space.

Great cover design needs to do a lot of things, from grabbing the reader's attention to engaging them on an emotional level that suggests the tone and style of the work, plus showcasing the potential quality of the book itself–all within a tiny almost-postage stamp sized image on a digital bookstore web page.

The main goal of every book cover is to generate excitement and attract attention. Think of the millions of potential readers that will only know your work by a quick glance at your cover. With millions of books for readers to choose from, the first "sales pitch" is the cover. If it is not striking enough to draw attention, it will be passed over for something more interesting in the browser window.

Marketing begins with your cover

As a professional marketer it pains me to say this: A brilliant cover is the absolute best tool in your future marketing arsenal. You can have the most amazing marketing plan, incredible reviews and blurbs, even a giant budget. But it will be all for naught if your cover doesn't do its job. It's your anchor point for all of your promotions, a graphical symbol of your book. Creating something that stops people in their tracks or on their browsers requires a special talent.

And chances are, Mr. or Ms. Author, you ain't got it. I mean no offense by that remark, but it takes the unique skills of a professional cover artist to achieve this. I have confidence that you'll recognize when your cover design has reached that lofty level. But knowing and doing are two different things. Book cover creation is an art form unto itself. It's different from simply drawing or painting, or even general graphic design. And digital cover design for eBooks is its own separate area.

Let me put it this way: How many good books have you read that were written by designers? Why should designing be any less a specialized skill?

Just like we discovered with editing, it pays to get cover design help. A recent Writer's Digest study shows that the most successful self-published authors hire professional cover designers. In fact, over 63% of authors surveyed who earned over $25,000 on their last book had design help.

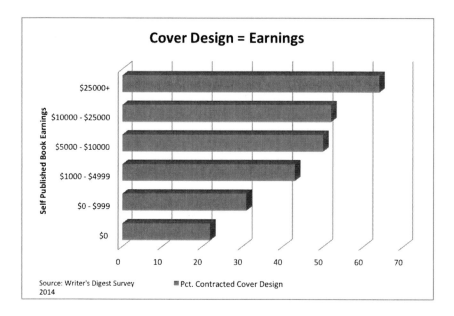

Finding your professional designer

As with our previous search for editing help, there are plenty of freelance book cover artists to be found online. It's a matter of matching the best artist in your genre with the price point you can afford. Before you go designer shopping, keep these things in mind:

Genre specific – Make sure the prospective designer works with your genre. The needs of a romance novel cover are different from the action adventure genre. Visit their portfolio to make sure they're up to designing for your niche.

Designs for the designer – How does the designer design for him/herself? Is the designer's website professionally designed? If the website doesn't look professional then how can you trust that the book covers will?

Reference check – Take the time to really check out their references. Talk with the authors they've worked with in the past. Ask if the designer is easy to work with, open to ideas, reliable (responsive and meets deadlines), and are the authors happy with the services rendered and the final product?

Do they do digital – This is critically important if you're going the eBook route. Make sure you see the designers' eBook cover designs. Subtle design that looks incredible at 9" x 6" will be crunched and squashed down to a measly few centimeters in Amazon thumbnails.

Designers are readers, too. When you're talking to prospective graphic designers, make sure they have experience in book design specifically. Book design has its own conventions that require a different approach from the design of other kinds of media or publications. Ask them what their favorite books are, which designs they admire and which of their own projects they most enjoyed working on. Their answers to your questions about other books will say a lot about the design work they do.

A few different approaches

Authors without the resources of traditional publishers and their legions of designers are left to their own devices. Often the first stop in finding help is online directories, forums or message boards. But this time-consuming option often yields few results. As we've already discovered, finding a freelance editor using online sources certainly presents a challenge. But to me it's much tougher to search and find a cover artist using Internet ads or design sites. That might seem strange considering the Internet allows you to easily view samples produced by designers around the world. Compare that kind of explicit sampling to those of editors; unless you have a specific before-and-after editing comparison, it's hard to know his or her exact handiwork.

It comes down to comfort level and familiarity. As a writer I pretty much know when an editor has had their way with my work. The improvement is undeniable. I don't have some same advantages in terms of design. Is Cover A better than Cover B? Or even Cover C? It's truly subjective and so I'm not content on a conventional search. I need something much more interactive – even iterative – to recommend.

Let's start with a company I just came across – 99designs (www.99designs.com). It's a graphic design crowd sourcing platform. Here's how it works: You create a "contest" where you describe your project and your budget. Designers who have signed up for the website compete by sending in designs that match your requirements. At time I'm writing this almost 900,000 designers are in the 99designs community. You can review all of the "contest entries" and if you like what you see, you can communicate with specific designers to help them fine-tune their entries.

Finally, when you get a book cover that's perfect for your needs, you choose the winner and pay them the "prize money". The benefit is obvious – you'll basically get an entire team of graphic designers to work on your book cover, and they'll likely come up with ideas that you may not have even thought of.

Also, you never have to worry about getting stuck with a design you don't like. If none of the designs meets your fancy, you don't have to choose a winner.

Book design contests at 99designs start at $299 but can go up the scale to over $1,199 if you so choose. That may seem a little pricey but the company offers 100% money back if you don't get a design you like, so there's no risk of paying for a design you don't love.

A similar site is Bibliocrunch (www.bibliocrunch.com). It's a little less structured than 99designs but still puts you in control of the process from end to end. On BiblioCrunch, professionals can sign up as an author, designer, editor, copy editor, publisher or reader. You can post your job description with your desired budget. Authors who can be specific about what they're looking for, the kinds of skills needed and your exact expectations in terms of budget and timeline have been very pleased with their results. They have a pricing guideline to help price out the job. One key feature of Bibliocrunch is the rating and review system where designers, and other professionals, are given testimonials on their work.

There are other design websites that offer the same basic service and setup. You can post your ad for exactly what you want on freelancer websites like Elance. com, oDesk.com or DesignCrowd.com. One that I've used recently on another project was Guru.com (www.guru.com).

I was fortunate in that I know a great designer who just so happens to work for my company. She's designed all of the guides I've written and I asked her to create the cover for this book. If I wasn't so fortunate to have design resources, I would strongly consider these types of freelancer websites. You're completely in control of your entire project, including the price and timeline. You'll receive bids for the project from freelancers all over the country and the world who are willing to work on your projects and on your terms. It would be very interesting to have multiple designers bidding on the opportunity to take my project, especially when I don't have to haggle over pricing. Plus most of these sites have some kind of guarantee for their services. A site like Elance, for instance, doesn't release payment to the artist until they know the client is happy with the results of a project.

A few more ideas for your designer search

Go for your favorite – Look up the designers of the book covers you admire. Designers are usually credited on a book's cover or copyright page. Make a list of the designers of great-looking books in the same subject category as yours and research them. While some designers will be employed full-time by publishers and won't do freelance work, some will be freelancers and might take on self-published titles, especially if the work is in line with other projects they've undertaken. When you search, look for books published by small or medium-sized publishers, because they often use freelance designers who work for a variety of clients, rather than in-house designers who work exclusively for them.

Student discounts – You can find very talented design students – and even professors who do freelance design – at design schools. Contact department heads or administrators at reputable design schools to inquire about locating job boards or finding other ways of reaching out to students and staff for potential freelance work.

Think local – If you're starting from scratch in your search for a designer, why not do an online search for book designers in your local area? That way, you can have the added benefit of meeting in-person once in a while, which can help to establish a good rapport.

The billboard for your book

We all agree a great book cover is vital. But it still makes sense to review the facts so that you can make some quick decisions about who will create your book cover. For every author – self-published or otherwise – visibility is key. Generating visibility takes time and persistence and includes everything from a Twitter feed to book reviews. But a great book cover can generate more buzz and visibility than most social marketing plans and even the best of endorsements.

Your cover is not only a billboard for the book, but in reality, the first page of your story. It's the readers' initial glimpse of all that you have to reveal in the next few hundred pages to come. Let's assume your book is a fictional novel of some genre. Before the reader even gets inside the book, your cover can communicate the mood and style of the tale inside. Some things are obvious at this point. A dark cover, with lots of shadow, can suggest a horror novel, while a bright white cover with clouds could suggest a motivational textbook. Bright blood red brings murder and mayhem to mind.

These seem fairly obvious, of course, and in some ways run counter to one of the important book marketing concepts preached everywhere: Your book needs to stand out to be discovered. And yet….go into your local Barnes & Noble today and see how many successful authors are not following these unwritten "rules". Though obvious, these simple cues are accepted to be the established visual cues for potential readers. They've probably read many books in this genre that have these same telltale colors, textures or backgrounds. After having good experiences reading books that are decorated in such a consistent style, the covers now go straight to emotions of the reader, engaging them on a deeper level. That means not just securing a book sale, but setting the stage for whether or not they will like the book in the first place.

Through both subtle imagery and explicit text and graphics, your cover will create preconceptions in a reader's mind about what the characters or the setting look like. That has its pros and cons. If you fail to hit the mark, your cover design may not match the reader's ideas. Books in some genres – romance and erotica especially – need to have the faces – and bodies – to go with the names. Many books are sold almost solely on the strength of an appealing model or striking face. The goal for those book covers is to entice readers in the same way as they might entice each other as characters in the story.

Cover design 101

What goes into a cover design? Well, there's the title with an eye-catching image or two. The name of the author is important, as is information on the spine. Maybe a blurb or two on the back cover. That's just the bare minimum, of course, so let's cover some of the more important elements for your book cover:

Designing a postage stamp – Assuming that you're creating an eBook cover, remember how your image will be viewed online. It's a tiny rectangle, surrounded by hundreds of other rectangles. So your design needs to be bold and overt, not subtle. For instance if you choose a curly script font because your book is a historical romance, make sure it's readable even at thumbnail size. The same goes for your main image – it needs to be recognizable at a thumbnail size.

The image on your book cover should be something that can be processed quickly. If people have to squint to figure out that that green shape is a dragon, then you're going to lose potential readers. Lack of real estate means that cropping your images will be extremely important. You can be working with the most beautiful image in the world, but if it's not placed so it creates the maximum impact, then it's not going to do you any good.

Art that's appropriate – The images used on your cover can create a visual shorthand for a book's genre. An image of a man flying a WWII airplane signals that you're probably not looking at a science fiction novel. Most people, including designers, use stock images, since the cost of custom art is so high, and there are many stock image websites out there that provide literally millions of images. Make sure the image you select effectively conveys the essence of your book.

While great art is a key element to the cover, you should avoid the most obvious or clichéd types of main images. Don't try to tell the whole story with the cover artwork. Rather, garner a potential reader's interest and make them want to know more. Keep it simple on the front cover; it's the back cover's job to summarize the plot or house those coveted blurbs you've collected.

Of course, if you do have the skills and experience to design your own book cover or for some reason you still don't want to hire a professional, here are some good places to look for images that could look good on your cover and don't cost a lot:

http://www.bigstockphoto.com/search/category/abstract/

http://www.istockphoto.com/

http://www.stockphotography.com/

http://www.stockphotos.com/

http://www.acclaimimages.com/

http://www.gettyimages.com/

Easy to buy = easy to read – Your cover typography needs to be very easy on the eye. Sure, it's tempting to go crazy with stylized type so your book stands out from the crowd, but such creativity comes with a cost. Readers with a choice of thousands of other books simply won't be bothered to decipher your odd typefaces. With a little work you can have it both ways, with type that's both interesting and legible.

It's generally recommended that you use at most two faces – a sans serif and serif face can provide a good contrast. Most of the time the title should be bigger than the author's name, unless you're already a household name. The title should be the first element to help sell your book. Title, name and blurb are the minimum you need, plus a tagline and any review quotes that you'd like to feature on the cover.

Clean and uncluttered – White space is a book designer's best friend. Even the tiny book cover designs created for online sales need some kind of "empty" areas to give the eye a rest. They also provide a cue as to where you should be focusing your attention. That means you'll need to avoid the temptation to put blurbs all over the cover or make the text so big that it overpowers the background image. Sometimes a subhead is necessary, but keep in mind that it probably won't show up in a thumbnail.

Colors that complement, not clash – There isn't one specific color that works best for all genres of books. As noted above, some subject matters demand different color palettes. Choose black, red, and white for thrillers or mysteries, for example. Conversely, romances often have softer, warmer palettes in shades of pastels. But in every case the colors chosen should work together. Also, certain genres tend to have predominant color palettes.

Beauty, as they say, is in the eye of the beholder. Not everyone is going to agree on what makes a great cover, since people's taste varies so greatly. However, if you keep these simple rules in mind as you're designing a cover, you're much more likely to create something that works as an effective sales tool for your book. Also, don't be afraid to look around for design inspiration – there are thousands of talented designers whose covers can help guide you as you determine what works best for your book.

There's so much to think about and consider. For me it's less about design rules or established practice. I know what I like. And – as Supreme Court Justice Oliver Wendell Holmes said about pornography – I know it when I see it. One way I collect these visuals is to save them the images into a folder on my computer. Other authors I talk with use Pinterest to create boards to post ideas. In fact I think you should do two: One for great cover designs and the other for designs or styles to avoid. You can start pinning anytime so when you are ready to book your cover designer, you have already put thought into this. There are some excellent book design-related websites that can provide inspiration and even some ideas about designers to contact. The Book Cover Archive (www.bookcoverarchive.com) is a great resource. At the bottom of their home page you will find links to other book design sites they recommend.

With varying price points and a multitude of resources online, self-published authors have more options every day. Whether they opt to crowdsource, outsource, or go it alone, the goal is clear – create a visual that matches the quality consumers have come to expect from the industry giants. This begins with the cover and gives every author a chance to find their audience.

I avoided the whole "judge a book by its cover" thing at the start. But I can't stop myself from another cliché to end this section:

You only have one chance to make a first impression, so make sure your book cover creates the impression you intended.

Step 6 – Digital or Analog?

eBooks? Printed Books? What are your options?

TIMELINE: 1 WEEK

> *Prose is architecture, not interior decoration.*
> - Ernest Hemingway

If we're still on our 6-week schedule, you should have your freshly edited manuscript ready to go. And go-time it is.

Up to this point, I've stayed neutral on a lot of the topics covered. These are your decisions, impacting your literary career, and this book is all about informing and helping you make good decisions for writing career.

But I can't in good conscience steer you toward what could be a bad decision. I've talked to a lot of writers in this same exact place, and I've listened to their stories about how they published their very first book. I make a point of asking them, "If you could go back in time and do it all again, what would you do differently?" And one thing is mentioned over and over. Hearing this over the last few years, some choices become very obvious to professionals in the publishing business.

But for the record we'll stick to the script. This week's decision: Should you produce your manuscript in a printed book? Or should you opt for an eBook?

This is your decision, but here is my opinion based on all the experiences mentioned above: The answer is yes. Authors in the 21st century need both. If your goal is to make money and attract readers, you need both the digital – online – and analog – offline – versions of your books. In my mind there's not really much to debate. But we'll give it a try anyway.

In this chapter we will:

- Examine recent studies about readers and their reading habits.
- Examine the pros and cons of each format, starting with the perspective of the reader.
- Cover some necessary technical information about file conversions for eBook and formatting tips.

Reading is alive, well...and going online.

We learned early in this book how Americans still love to read. While most still enjoy leafing through the pages of printed books, a growing number of readers are turning to the digital version. The popularity of eBooks is rising, with millions of readers enjoying new levels of convenience, portability, access, and affordability with their Kindles, iPads, Nooks, tablets, smartphones, and other devices.

But now we're going to break it down farther. What age groups have turned to eBooks? Just about everyone, from the young to the young-at-heart. Not surprisingly, the early adapters were in the middle age brackets that could best afford the often pricey devices. As eReader, tablet and cell phone prices dropped, so too did the age group that made up the latest increase in eBook adoption.

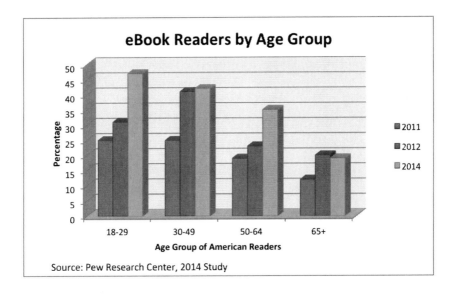

eBook Readers by Age Group

Source: Pew Research Center, 2014 Study

It's not time to clear off those bookshelves just yet, but the sales numbers for eBooks in the last few years show where the publishing industry is heading — and fast. The latest research shows that as of mid-2014, almost 50% of all Americans owned some kind of eReader device. That's a jump of 37% in less than three years. By the time you're reading this, it's bound to be up another couple of points. And that doesn't even count readers — including me — who are using smartphone apps to read their favorite books.

It's almost ancient history now, but you can point to two events that really triggered the explosive growth of eBooks starting in mid-2010:

Product – Apple introduced its revolutionary iPad in April 2010, selling over 3 million devices in the first 80 days. Just over four years later, total iPad sales worldwide have soared to over 200 million. iPad made consuming content easier and more fun! While many other companies have produced their own tablets, iPads remain the king of the category.

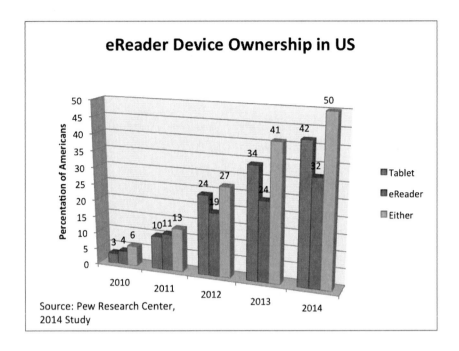

eReader Device Ownership in US

Source: Pew Research Center, 2014 Study

Price – The lifecycle pricing of every electronic device has always decreased over time. But price levels for eReaders have been on an express elevator heading toward the basement. Starting in 2010, Amazon reduced the price of its best-selling Kindle 2 to $189, in response to Barnes & Noble's new low-priced Nook offering. Suddenly reading devices were available to millions of eager readers and the gold rush was on! Now a basic Kindle can be had for $79. eReading has come to the masses.

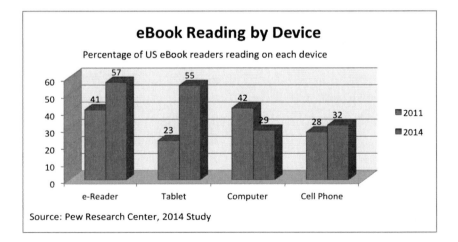

eBook Reading by Device

Percentage of US eBook readers reading on each device

Source: Pew Research Center, 2014 Study

Just like that favorite book you can tuck under your arm or in your bag, Americans love the portability of eBooks. Use of the slim eReaders and Tablets has boomed over the last three years, and as cell phone screens are growing larger, more readers are also using those devices. Meanwhile, computers are the only form of electronic device showing a decline in reading use.

While the Pew research was restricted to American reading habits, it's well understood that the eBook wave is crashing against foreign shores as well. Europe has been slower to take to eBooks but the growth curve is now steep in the EU. In China, there are numerous eReaders available, but most of the digital reading public reads on their over one billion mobile phones. Amazon has exported their Kindle Reader to every corner of the planet.

Books are books, digital or analog

The rise of eBooks and the readers that display them has caused the media to say that printed books are dying or are already dead. This, of course, is not really the case. If beautiful leather-bound books or paperback books were dead, what would be the use of book stores? And as you'll shortly learn in our last chapter, those stores are very much alive and well. Yet another example of the media reporting without research.

The Pew Research study clearly shows that book sales are shifting. Many more books are being purchased as eBooks for many reasons including cost. However, many books are still being purchased on paper, and bookstores are still making profits (albeit smaller ones).

For many types of books, the printed option is still the better one, notwith-standing advances in the realm of iPad and Kindle. The categories with little comparative digital advantage (except possibly price) are:

- Books where typography and design is of utmost important. Some examples might be design books, hardcover gifts, and the ever-popular "coffee table" books.

- Books with many pictures such as cookbooks, atlases, photo books.

- Books where durability is important, including cookbooks and children's books.

- Textbooks where readers often annotate with notes.

- Any book where owning the printed 'artifact' is more important than the printed word. These would be first editions, limited edition books and signed books. The collectible book market is still thriving.

- Conversely, there are some types of books especially suited for an eReader:

- Any books that are strictly text only. That includes novels or non-fiction books with few pictures.

- Books that are linked directly to websites, with html links and cross references.

The reader's perspective

Let's start our discussion of the pros and cons of book formats with our reader in mind. After all, finding readers who will buy your books is the point of this exercise for the vast majority of folks reading this book. The readers' needs must be considered in your decision.

Starting with the time-honored paper book, this classic presentation offers many advantages:

- They're easily obtainable (Bookstores are everywhere).
- They're very portable.
- They don't normally cause significant eyestrain.

Okay, that much was obvious. But there's more, especially when you compare them directly to their digital cousin, the eBook. I'll save most of these for the "cons" list for eBooks, but one needs to be highlighted:

- Paper books don't require an eReader. While ownership is growing at a rapid clip, you'll still be excluding potential readers if you go eBook only. Another factor to bear in mind is that paper books don't need power to function. They can be read anywhere with sufficient light, and are perfect travelling companions for exactly this reason.

The obvious cons are:

- Paper books are bulky and heavy. Carrying more than 2-3 around can become a chore.

- If you make notes in them, those notes are there to stay (Yes, even pencil. You can always see the imprints, even if you erase every last shred of graphite).

- They're more expensive than the typical eBook. Unless you're buying all your reading material at used book stores, printed books are between 50 to 100% more expensive.

As we've seen, eBook readership is on the rise. Here are just a few of the reasons readers are turning to the Kindle, Nook and other devices for that favorite book:

- Instant access. Let's say you just heard a report on the TV about a wonderful new book. You can either jump in your car, drive to the closest bookstore and hope they have it in stock, or simply go to your favorite online bookstore, search for the new book and download it almost instantly.

- The newest devices make reading a pleasure, with zoom functions, letter resizing, and so forth.

- They're portable. You can carry hundreds of books on one device.

- They're much more environmentally friendly. You don't have to kill a few trees for each book, and let's not even talk about the ink. Recycling only goes so far.

The disadvantages of eBooks start with the requirement for some kind of hardware. Yes, they've come down in price over the past few years. Still, it's a hurdle for a reader to jump over. Some other factors include:

- Eye strain. Long periods spent in front of a computer are healthy for nobody.

- Readers require a power supply of some type. Battery life will continue to improve over the coming years but it's still an issue.

- You have some issues of portability. Are you going to take your nifty reading device to a sandy beach?

The writer's case for eBooks

It's fairly easy to understand why authors have turned to eBooks as the best alternative to jumpstart their writing career:

Low cost to create - The cost to produce eBooks ranges from extremely cheap – meaning free – to relatively cheap. Yes, you have to convert your manuscript files – such as Microsoft Word, Text Files or PDFs – into different formats to be able to be used on eReaders. (More about this later in the chapter.) But file conversion costs by providers are coming down, and the DIY options are getting better every day.

The low cost of eBooks allows authors to consider new options for presenting their writing to the world. Authors are publishing "singles" or short stories on the web to gauge reader reactions to a subject matter or genre. Or they're breaking up their existing work and serializing chapters of the book. Again, you can use this idea to trot out new ideas. Established authors are using it for a far different reason – maximizing sales. I encourage you to read the exploits of the aforementioned JK Konrath on his blog, "The Newbie's Guide To Publishing". He's done an amazing job in repackaging these existing novels into segments like this. Or he's bundling digital books together to offer readers a different buying option. You could never attempt this kind of innovative merchandising with a printed book!

Low cost to distribute – Just as it's cheap to get your eBook converted into useable files, it's just as inexpensive to get your eBook distributed across the globe. You can go direct to Amazon, Apple's iBooks, Barnes & Noble and many others, or use a low cost service like BookBaby to put you in all those stores and many more.

Ability to distribute – Unless you're involved in a traditional publishing deal, eBooks are the usually the best option for any kind of book distribution. Yes, there are plenty of POD (print on demand) types of opportunities for printed book sales, but these are usually expensive and less than satisfactory for most independent authors.

Available everywhere, anytime – Global distribution is within the reach of every author. Readers can find your eBook in Tasmania at 2 am local time, and everyplace else that has an Internet connection.

Fastest to the marketplace – Like the title of this book claims, your work will be in eBook stores in a matter of weeks. Once your manuscript is edited and your cover is finished, eBook production and distribution takes just a few weeks, even if you go through a third-party distributor such as BookBaby.

Add multimedia – You can't link to a video from the pages of a printed book. From the early days of the Kindle, publishing visionaries have hailed the eBook as the gateway to a true multimedia experience for authors. It hasn't come to pass in any meaningful way just yet. The technology is available, of course. The challenge is producing the kind of video and audio content that can be matched with the book. I think this is going to remain a niche or fringe aspect of eBooks for the foreseeable future. Most authors I talk to are interested in – and only good at – writing. They aren't going to take the time to produce the other kinds of media that will unlock the potential of this format.

Last and certainly least:

Best payout – Here's what every author is waiting to read. You'll make the most money on each eBook sold. We discussed this previously in the Pathway chapter. That's a stone cold lock, assuming you are taking the self-publishing route, of course, and you don't have a publisher who controls your book.

Amazon returns as much as 70% of the sales price back to authors going direct. To get the highest return, your book has to be priced within a certain range and must fit other criteria. But the vast majority of books can qualify for this generous return. And most of the other eBook stores like Apple and Barnes & Noble return the same percentage of net sales.

As discussed earlier in the Marketing chapter, your profits will be influenced heavily by your pricing strategies. No matter how successful you eventually become, it will always be a tradeoff between profit and popularity. The lower the price, the more readers you'll get. That's going to be true if you're as famous as Hugh Howey.

Minority Report

And now for other side of the argument, thin as it may be. There are a few cons to eBooks.

eBooks are not for everyone – The Pew research illustrates that eBook readership is still far behind printed books. There is a sizable population of readers who vow to remain paper-based consumers. Many enjoy the tactile feel of paper and ink. But how long will that last?

Hardware not included – Must have an eReader, tablet, or smartphone. Not every one of your potential readers has a Kindle, iPad or other device. But smartphones are being used

Not optimal format for every book – As previously mentioned, graphic-heavy books or textbooks are not ideal formats for eBooks. That's not to say these volumes are excluded from the eBook world. Most of these kinds of books require a processed called "Fixed Layout" to work best on digital reading devices. The same is true for many children's books. The conversion process is often very expensive and takes time to create by professional digital designers.

In praise of print

A few brief words to illustrate the obvious advantages of the ink-on-paper format:

Still the one – The media's call that books are dead is obviously in error. The research clearly shows that printed books remain the choice for most readers. That's not going to change anytime soon. I can see a time when eBook and printed book format preferences begin to even out. It makes the case for doing both that much stronger, of course.

You're legit! There's nothing like a freshly printed book to tell the world: "I'm an author!"

Accessible – No eReader needed to consume this old world technology.

Ready to be personalized – Authors can sign them and give to readers. On the other side of the pages, your readers can easily make notes or highlight special passages.

Not fastest but still fast – Thanks to modern technology, you can have books printed in as fast as a week. And that doesn't even count POD (print on demand) situations that can be printed after initial set up …well, on demand!

Collectable – Ever seen a first edition eBook?

Now that there's a choice, not every self-published author is choosing to have printed books made. They're swept up in the wave of technology and either forget or ignore (or maybe aren't aware of) the huge number of readers that would prefer to read a printed book. I personally think it's a mistake to go only one direction in terms of a format, as I'll cover in a few pages. But these are the issues cited by authors who decide against printing:

Costly to produce – There's no question that having printed books produced is going to be an investment. While short-run and POD brings the total cost down, there's still a significant upfront cost to printing your own book. Self-published authors can recoup this investment by getting placement in local bookstores, selling their books on their own websites and other ways. But they might also be simply a cost of doing business. For instance, people who do public speaking engagements need a book to support their efforts.

Hard to sell, offline or online – We've already talked about the difficulty of self-published authors getting distribution for printed books. And it's not very easy to sell them online either. Certainly you can market these products on your own website and maybe Amazon Marketplace. But you also have to package and ship the product direct. Is playing shipping clerk the best use of your time?

There are distribution deals to be found for self-published authors, but many are very suspect or outright scams.

Take my advice just this once

As I warned the beginning of this chapter, I have a strong opinion about your choice between eBooks and printed books. And it's this:

It's not a choice. You need both at this – and every stage – of your writing career. I'm not saying this as someone who wants to sell you an eBook and/or printed books. I'm saying this as a fellow author. As soon as this manuscript is finished, I'm getting both.

But the most compelling argument I can make regarding this situation comes not as a writer but as a marketer. I won't restate any of the points presented above to make my case. I'll simply restate one of the cardinal rules of marketing. Above everything else – messaging, positioning, pricing – there's one undeniable commandment for everyone selling something:

Make it easy to buy. Do all that you can to help the consumer open his or her wallet. Quite simply, that means you need to offer your readers the chance to find your work online in eBooks and offline in printed books. Anything less is handicapping your literary efforts, limiting your readership and restricting your financial rewards.

Enough said.

You mean I can't just use my .doc file?

Most everyone knows what an eBook is by now. But a lot of authors still don't know much more than the name. Relatively few know how they are created, or even what they look like on an eReader. So we'll do a little eBook file conversion 101 here to bring you up to speed.

No matter the content or genre, your manuscript has one final hurdle to jump before it is eReader-ready: You'll need to have your manuscript converted to ePUB and .mobi format.

Of the two, ePub is the dominant format in terms of a near-universal acceptance of the file type. From the iPad to the Nook, almost every eReader uses some variation of the ePub file in which to display eBooks.

So what is .mobi, and why do we even mention it if almost all eReaders use ePub? That's because the one company that uses it has a pretty important place in the publishing industry. It's a little organization called Amazon. To make your eBook available for the Kindle, you'll need to make sure you have a .mobi file.

With your freshly edited manuscript in hand, it's best if you review the following formatting guidelines. Whether you're doing the conversion yourself or having a professional conversion house take care of the job (see sidebar), you can go a long way toward making the process easier by making some simple fixes if necessary:

- Use basic text files to upload. eBook formatting works best when authors can supply original files in .doc, .html or .txt file formats.

- Don't use tabs or the space bar to format paragraphs or individual lines. Use the format paragraph menu or the alignment buttons in the toolbar of your text-editing program.

- Use standard fonts for your document, like Times New Roman or Courier New. Don't use very large or very small font sizes. Use 12pt. font size for body text and 14-18pt. for chapter titles.

- Resize large images to 300 pixels high if you would like them to display in-line with text.

- Do all image resizing work outside of the document, then reinsert them before saving. All images must be in .png, .jpg, or .tif format, 72 dpi, and in RGB color mode.

- Don't wrap text around images. All images (except full-page images) should be set "in-line" with text.

eBook file conversion – a necessary evil

It's just about your last fork in the road for digital publishing. Do you want a professional file conversion house to produce the necessary digital files for Amazon, Apple and the rest? Or do you want to save the expense and do it yourself?

Lots of authors have gone down the DIY road and found success. You'll find a lot of great information on websites, author forums, and more to walk you through it. For instance, if you want to sell your book only in Amazon's Kindle Store, you can convert your Word file for free by submitting it yourself to Amazon's Kindle Direct Publishing.

To reach other stores, including Apple's iBooks and Barnes & Noble, converting your Word file into ePUB isn't for everyone. With the technology, standards, and best practices for eBook conversion constantly in flux, it's tough for authors to stay abreast of all the latest developments.

I recommend leaving the technical details to the experts. You can hire designers or conversion houses to do the work. As long as it's a simple text-heavy book it's not very expensive. My company, BookBaby, does it for as little as $99 — and your book will look great on all the different eReaders in the marketplace.

Since I've already said this chapter is about sharing my opinion, I'll do it one more time: Writers should be doing what they do best – write. Hire someone else to do the technical heavy lifting. If BookBaby is your choice – great – but there are plenty of options out there.

Time to publish

A review of our journey from manuscript to marketplace

TIMELINE: AFTER 6 WEEKS

We are all apprentices in a craft where no one ever becomes a master.
—Ernest Hemingway

We've come a long way in six short weeks.

- In Week 1 we made it official – the book is finally done. Yes, really. It passed all of the "tests" that we've covered. You're confident that every word you've written is perfect as is…

- …Or not! You bought into the notion that editing was an essential step in Week 2. Without a trained, critical eye reading your words, all you have is a raw manuscript. You might have decided to use some of the DIY ideas I've offered. Or maybe you've hired the perfect editor for your genre or niche. Either way, your prose will be taken to new heights.

- While your book was being edited in Week 3, you considered the two main paths to the marketplace – Self-publishing or the Traditional route.

- Week 4 saw us covering some basic book marketing ideas, broken down in a different way: Book Merchandising and Promotion. Both are important and well within your reach. This is often the hardest part of the journey for authors but now you've got a good basic roadmap to follow.

- We discussed the importance of book cover design in Week 5, and you were convinced to seek professional help. You can't leave this oh-so-critical part of your book product to your brother-in-law who went to art school 17 years ago.

- And when your edited manuscript made its way back to you in Week 6, we discussed the pros and cons of eBooks vs. Printed Books – plus covered some basic formatting guidelines for eBook publishing.

Whew, that's a forced march to the marketplace. Of course it might not be a 6-week journey – it might be 16 if your book needs more editing. Or more time to consider some of the other steps I've outlined. And that's fine. The exact timeline doesn't matter nearly as much as the need to produce a terrific book. And by "terrific book" I mean everything we've reviewed here: edited content, brilliant cover, format, distribution and marketing plan.

For some of you reading this book, it will be a linear journey, a straight line toward global distribution of your well-chosen words and pictures. For others there could be curves or obstacles in your path. These final six tasks and decision points discussed in this book have waylaid countless would-be authors. There are countless writers who remain on the sidelines, holding the manuscript they've written maybe 3, 5 or 10 years ago. And it's a darned shame – most of the hard work is already done. They've got the content but lack the confidence or information to take it out of the top drawer or file on the hard drive. It might be what they call analysis paralysis – a term we use when people have too many options to choose between and they simply shut down. Or it could be the exact opposite – writers don't know where to turn to get help. This is ultimately what I hope this book will accomplish – to inform, clarify, and motive writers to get in the game.

Your next move

Here's the part where I politely show you the door. Nudge you from the nest. Choose your metaphor but it's almost time for you put this book down and make a decision:

If you've chosen to self-publish, you're all ready to go. Whether you choose our company, BookBaby, to take care of your publishing needs, or you choose to go direct to Amazon, you've put yourself in near-perfect position to begin your publishing career on the fast track.

If instead you've chosen the traditional route of seeking an agent, your chances for success have been enhanced by the work you've done to prepare your manuscript for careful scrutiny by publishers. Good luck with that journey.

But there's another direction you can take your book, and it's the one I recommend most strongly – more so than anything else in this book:

Do both. At the very same time. It's called Hybrid Publishing, and more than a few mainstream authors are using this approach. Now the same path is available to you, Mr. or Ms. Starting Author.

A couple of chapters back we talked about the pros and cons of Self- or Traditional Publishing. So what if neither feels quite right? You like some aspects of both models. What if you want to do both?

That's the answer – do both. You really have nothing to lose at this stage of your career, so try as many things as possible to jumpstart your writing career. This dual model of publishing that is just now starting to emerge is a combination of self-publishing and traditional publishing that empowers both authors, and quite frankly, even publishers.

Hybrid publishing is very difficult to pin down because it's dynamic. There are many different ways to approach this kind of strategy. As you've learned for yourself, there are clear steps, benefits, and drawbacks to the distinctly separate models of self-publishing and traditional publishing. By pursuing a hybrid publishing strategy, authors take what they want from each model that best suits their own situation. The more recent development to the hybrid publishing approach is that most publishers encourage and applaud this course. Traditional publishers gain from writers' own trailblazing efforts, making for a tailored, innovative approach to publishing, which offers mutual benefits to all parties involved.

Your Hybrid Publishing game plan

While it's safe to that say that it's neither self-publishing nor traditional publishing but a combination of the two, hybrid publishing is difficult to define because there are so many possible variations. And that's the beauty of this approach. Every author's situation is different. Hybrid can be a one size fits all kind of approach. One more bonus: This approach can be applied not just to a single project but to an entire career.

Take a look at some of the most common examples of hybrid publishing strategy:

- Author 1 – His career started with traditionally published books, but watching the rise of self-publishing, he decides to try it for himself. From there, the author publishes some books traditionally and self-publishes others. The previously-mentioned Hugh Howey is a perfect example of this strategy.

- Author 2 – She has self-published several books and is picked up by a traditional publisher. She established an author's platform and attracted the attention of an agent and/or publisher with her own marketing and sales. As an aside, I have a member of my own staff who has gone down this exact path. He and his illustrator partner signed a three-book contract with a traditional publisher after putting it out through BookBaby.

- Author 3 – They might get a traditional book deal for printed book publishing but continue to self-publish eBooks, retaining all digital rights and royalties. More commonly, authors – or even estates of authors – are using ancient pre-Internet contract language to assume digital rights. Recent court rulings have favored these "jailbreaks" away from the grip of legacy publishers.

And there are a dozen other possible scenarios that can employ both models at once. Simply put, these new hybrid models are changing the face of publishing. So what are the benefits?

I've mentioned above how Hybrid Publishing is a win-win for all concerned, including the traditional publishers. The legacy publishers benefit from hybrid publishing because they can sign authors who have already self-published and established an audience or are in the process. It's like the National Football League depending on the college system to vet the next stars of the game. That's a lower-risk investment for the publisher because they know the books should sell to existing readers and fans. Even if the sales level isn't spectacular, they can better judge the appeal of your book's premise or topic when it's a real, tangible product and not just an empty pitch letter.

Like the NFL, it's not a complete given that these authors will be on the New York Times bestseller list. Sports fans remember Ryan Leaf, the can't-miss quarterback who came out the same year as perennial all-pro Peyton Manning. Leaf did miss, in a big way. And so will some of these authors tabbed by traditional publishers. It happens.

You may have noticed how the movie studios showing the latest films at the local Cineplex tend to like sequels, or movie premises that seem like a 'can't miss' proposition. Nowadays they rarely experiment with new, untested leading actors or actresses or try to cover subject matter that's far from traditional movie plot formulas. They simply can't risk $100 million misses. On a much smaller scale, every new author is a risk for a publishing house. There's no way to tell which books will make the bestseller lists and which ones will bomb. Mind you, we're not talking about $100 million dollar losses here, but as traditional publishers are getting weaker in our new publishing climate, they can ill afford any losing efforts.

Think about the process of publishing a book by a new author from the publisher's perspective: they have to hire a staff to read query letters, book excerpts, and full texts. They pay editors to review selected texts and decide whether they're worth publishing. They pay a team of editors, cover designers, book layout designers, printers, and distributors, all with absolutely no way of knowing if the book will find its audience. From a business perspective, that's a pretty risky model, especially when you consider the fact that most agents and editors admit they have no idea why some books make a splash while others sink to the bottom of the bargain bin.

There must be tremendous savings in paying someone to peruse self-published books online instead of using the traditional query process. Recruiters can sift through ratings and reviews, look at samples of texts, and determine the likely success they'll enjoy with certain authors. Meanwhile, authors who self-publish are honing both their writing and marketing skills on a smaller stage, so if and when they're picked up by a publisher, they have the proper experience to reach out to the broader audience that the publisher will expose them to. Like I said: It's a win-win.

Backed by the sales and or marketing efforts already put forth for any given self-published title, under this model it's less likely that a book or author will suffer low sales because there's already an audience ready, willing, and able to buy.

When authors self-publish, they earn a larger percentage of royalties as long as they price their books properly. With Amazon Kindle, for example, if you price your book between $2.99 and $9.99, your royalties are 70%. That's an awful lot compared to traditionally published authors, whose payments average between 6-11% for paperback and 17-25% for an eBook under the current payment schedules. As suggested in the examples above, authors who have already published traditionally can leverage their existing audience by self-publishing a few books and enjoying larger royalties on their self-published titles.

Or you can slice even thinner, like breakout author Hugh Howey. Howey got a print publishing deal and was able to keep his digital rights, which means he will continue to collect larger royalties on his eBooks (up to 70% for Kindle sales) than most traditionally published authors receive. His argument – and that of authors everywhere – is this: The expense of printing, distribution, and storage is non-existent for eBooks, so it makes sense for authors to keep a larger share of the royalties.

Is this the future?

Is hybrid publishing the future of the industry? Once you consider all of the issues and risk, does it really make sense for publishers to continue footing the expense of publishing new authors? Does it really make sense for authors to go through the long, often agonizing process of querying agents and publishers when they could be spending that same time getting their books into the marketplace? I'd answer both those questions with a resounding "no".

In terms of overall revenue and sales, self-publishing is still dwarfed by the mainstream publishers. Industry research shows that in 2011, self-publishing is thought to have drained roughly $100 million in revenue from the traditional trade publishing business — a drop in the bucket for the $14 billion business. But in 2012, that number is thought to have doubled. With the increasing success of self-published authors in hitting bestseller lists, the number should continue to go up.

But just when we start thinking the publishing industry is headed down one track, other new ideas seem to pop up. For now, though, hybrid publishing offers authors and publishers the best of both worlds. By lowering the risk for publishers and raising the earnings potential for authors, it's an ideal model for the here and now.

For the last words on the matter – and in this book – I turn to one of the most amazing success stories in the brief history of self-publishing. The aforementioned Hugh Howey decided to self-publish his post-apocalyptic thriller *Wool* as a 99-cent eBook on Amazon in July of 2011. Within just a few months it because one of the high ranking books on Amazon sci-fi best seller charts. Howey racked up 5,260 reviews while selling over 20,000 digital copies each month. Producers who were searching for the next Hunger Games franchise came courting. Howey somehow had the foresight – and fortitude – to turn down seven-figure figure offers from traditional publishers before finally reaching a six-figure, print-only deal with Simon & Schuster.

Howey participated on a panel on self-publishing that I moderated at a recent Book Expo America event, and he shared some interesting thoughts with me about how authors should decide their publishing path:

I think writers should ask themselves three questions:

1) *What does the author want from their writing career?*
2) *What are they willing to invest?*
3) *What should they expect?*

If an author wants a successful writing career (1), I would tell them they should be willing to invest many years and be willing to write and self-publish many books (2), all without expecting immediate material gain or adulation (3). If they persist, they stand a good chance of building an audience, improving their craft, and establishing a catalog of material that will be for sale for the rest of their lives and beyond.

If an author wants to write that one great book and see it in bookstores (1), they should perfect a single manuscript over however many years it takes (2) and they should expect very thin chances of ever seeing it published (3). But there's always that chance. It does happen.

If an author expects to go either route, publish a single book, and make a metric ton of money, they are certain to be disappointed. The cases on either side where this happens are literally one in several million. Pointing to these exceptions as goals is a path to ruin.

Howey is passionate about supporting his fellow authors, devoting much of his non-writing time these days to encouraging and supporting writers as they strive to realize just a fraction of his success. As someone who has benefitted from the self-publishing/technology revolution, Howey offers an interesting perspective on how writers have taken control of their careers:

Other artists have long had the ability to share their work on an open forum, hone their craft, and amass fans. This is how musicians build their brand and their careers. It's how comedians have operated. And fine artists to some degree.

As soon as the cost of production and distribution for stories dropped to zero, which is what the Internet and e-reading devices have done, it opened the world up to storytellers to be in charge of their own careers. How hard you are willing to work and how hard you are willing to study and practice are the only limiting factors these days. Luck will always play a part, but her role has been diminished.

I hope, too, that this book has help further shrunk the influence that blind luck has in your own success as a writer. If, however, you don't find your audience with this book, don't despair. Instead, do this: Go to the online group called Kboards. You'll soon find one board that includes a list of self-published authors, with high sellers listed first.

Look carefully at the list: You'll see that most of these high-selling authors have more than five books published. Some a lot more. To me, this says these authors mostly didn't get instant success. They found success as they published more and more books.

They wrote and wrote. Honed their craft. Found their voice. All the bromides about writing, which are actually true. So keep writing. Keep finishing.

Keeping taking those manuscripts to the marketplace!